W9-CPP-285

The Law of Obscenity and Pornography

Second Edition

Revised and Updated by
Margaret C. Jasper

Oceana's Legal Almanac Series:
Law for the Layperson

Oceana®

NEW YORK

OXFORD

UNIVERSITY PRESS

Oxford University Press, Inc., publishes works that further Oxford University's objective of excellence in research, scholarship, and education.

Copyright © 2009 by Oxford University Press, Inc.
Published by Oxford University Press, Inc.
198 Madison Avenue, New York, New York 10016

Oxford is a registered trademark of Oxford University Press
Oceana is a registered trademark of Oxford University Press, Inc.

Library of Congress Cataloging-in-Publication Data

Jasper, Margaret C.
The law of obscenity and pornography / by Margaret C. Jasper. – 2nd ed.
p. cm. — (Oceana's legal almanac series. Law for the layperson,
ISSN 1075-7376)
Includes bibliographical references.
ISBN 978-0-19-538617-2 ((hardback) : alk. paper)
1. Obscenity (Law)—United States—Popular works. 2. Pornography in popular culture—United States. 3. Pornography—Law and legislation—United States—Popular works. I. Title.
KF9444.J37 1996
345.73'0274 —dc22   2008053956

Note to Readers:

This publication is designed to provide accurate and authoritative information in regard to the subject matter covered. It is based upon sources believed to be accurate and reliable and is intended to be current as of the time it was written. It is sold with the understanding that the publisher is not engaged in rendering legal, accounting, or other professional services. If legal advice or other expert assistance is required, the services of a competent professional person should be sought. Also, to confirm that the information has not been affected or changed by recent developments, traditional legal research techniques should be used, including checking primary sources where appropriate.

(Based on the Declaration of Principles jointly adopted by a Committee of the American Bar Association and a Committee of Publishers and Associations.)

You may order this or any other Oxford University Press publication by visiting the Oxford University Press website at www.oup.com

To My Husband Chris

Your love and support

are my motivation and inspiration

To My Sons, Michael, Nick and Chris

-and-

In memory of my son, Jimmy

Table of Contents

ABOUT THE AUTHOR

MARGARET C. JASPER is an attorney engaged in the general practice of law in South Salem, New York, concentrating in the areas of personal injury and entertainment law. Ms. Jasper holds a Juris Doctor degree from Pace University School of Law, White Plains, New York, is a member of the New York and Connecticut bars, and is certified to practice before the United States District Courts for the Southern and Eastern Districts of New York, the United States Court of Appeals for the Second Circuit, and the United States Supreme Court.

Ms. Jasper has been appointed to the law guardian panel for the Family Court of the State of New York, is a member of a number of professional organizations and associations, and is a New York State licensed real estate broker operating as Jasper Real Estate, in South Salem, New York.

Margaret Jasper maintains a website at http://www.JasperLawOffice.com.

In 2004, Ms. Jasper successfully argued a case before the New York Court of Appeals, which gives mothers of babies who are stillborn due to medical negligence the right to bring a legal action and recover emotional distress damages. This successful appeal overturned a 26-year old New York case precedent, which previously prevented mothers of stillborn babies to sue their negligent medical providers.

Ms. Jasper is the author and general editor of the following Legal Almanacs:

AIDS Law (3d Ed.)

The Americans with Disabilities Act (2d Ed.)

Animal Rights Law (2d Ed.)

Auto Leasing

Bankruptcy Law for the Individual Debtor

Banks and Their Customers (3d Ed.)

Becoming a Citizen

Buying and Selling Your Home

Commercial Law

Consumer Rights Law

Co-ops and Condominiums: Your Rights and Obligations as an Owner

Credit Cards and the Law (2d Ed.)

Custodial Rights

Dealing with Debt

Dictionary of Selected Legal Terms (2d Ed.)

Drunk Driving Law

DWI, DUI and the Law

Education Law

Elder Law (2d Ed.)

Employee Rights in the Workplace (2d Ed.)

Employment Discrimination Under Title VII (2d Ed.)

Environmental Law (2d Ed.)

Estate Planning

Everyday Legal Forms

Executors and Personal Representatives: Rights and Responsibilities

Guardianship, Conservatorship and the Law

Harassment in the Workplace

Health Care and Your Rights Under the Law

Health Care Directives

Hiring Household Help and Contractors: Your Obligations Under the Law

Home Mortgage Law Primer (2d Ed.)

Hospital Liability Law (2d Ed.)

How to Change Your Name

How to Form an LLC

How to Protect Your Challenged Child

How to Start Your Own Business

Identity Theft and How to Protect Yourself

Individual Bankruptcy and Restructuring (2d Ed.)

Injured on the Job: Employee Rights, Worker's Compensation and Disability

Insurance Law

International Adoption

Juvenile Justice and Children's Law (2d Ed.)

Labor Law (2d Ed.)

Landlord-Tenant Law

Law for the Small Business Owner (2d Ed.)

The Law of Adoption

The Law of Attachment and Garnishment (2d Ed.)

The Law of Buying and Selling (2d Ed.)

The Law of Capital Punishment (2d Ed.)

The Law of Child Custody

The Law of Contracts

The Law of Copyright (2d Ed.)

The Law of Debt Collection (2d Ed.)

The Law of Alternative Dispute Resolution (2d Ed.)

The Law of Immigration (2d Ed.)

The Law of Libel and Slander

The Law of Medical Malpractice (2d Ed.)

The Law of No-Fault Insurance (2d Ed.)

The Law of Obscenity and Pornography (2d Ed.)

The Law of Patents

The Law of Personal Injury (2d Ed.)

The Law of Premises Liability (2d Ed.)

The Law of Product Liability (2d Ed.)

The Law of Special Education (2d Ed.)

The Law of Speech and the First Amendment

The Law of Trademarks

The Law of Violence Against Women (2d Ed.)

Lemon Laws

Living Together: Practical Legal Issues

Marriage and Divorce (3d Ed.)

Missing and Exploited Children: How to Protect Your Child

More Everyday Legal Forms

Motor Vehicle and Traffic Law

Nursing Home Negligence

Pet Law

Prescription Drugs

Privacy and the Internet: Your Rights and Expectations Under the Law (2d Ed.)

Probate Law

Protecting Your Business: Disaster Preparation and the Law

Real Estate Law for the Homeowner and Broker (2d Ed.)

Religion and the Law

Retirement Planning

The Right to Die (2d Ed.)

Rights of Single Parents

Small Claims Court

Social Security Law (2d Ed.)

Teenagers and Substance Abuse

Transportation Law: Passenger Rights & Responsibilities

Trouble Next Door: What to Do with Your Neighbor

Veterans' Rights and Benefits

Victim's Rights Law

Welfare: Your Rights and the Law

What If It Happened to You: Violent Crimes and Victims' Rights

What If the Product Doesn't Work: Warranties & Guarantees

Workers' Compensation Law (2d Ed.)

Your Child's Legal Rights: An Overview

Your Rights in a Class Action Suit

Your Rights as a Tenant

Your Rights Under the Family and Medical Leave Act

You've Been Fired: Your Rights and Remedies

INTRODUCTION

"I know it when I see it." Referring to obscenity, these famous words were spoken by U.S. Supreme Court Justice Potter Stewart in *Jacobellis v. Ohio (1964)*. If only it were as easy as Justice Potter stated, the courts would not be continually called upon to intervene and make such determinations.

The law of obscenity has evolved considerably since the first cases appeared in the courts. In part, this is due to the "new morality" that emerged in the late 1960s. Prior to that time, there were strict controls on the print and broadcast media. Censorship of images and language deemed obscene was the norm, particularly when there was a risk of exposure to minors. In fact, children of the 1950s were rarely exposed to anything remotely "indecent." For example, the parents on popular sitcoms slept in twin beds (e.g., *I Love Lucy* and *The Dick Van Dyke Show*), and profanity was virtually non-existent.

This Legal Almanac explores the law of obscenity and pornography. It sets forth the evolution of the relevant case law, including constitutional considerations and the various tests that the U.S. Supreme Court has devised to balance the regulation of obscenity and the First Amendment right to free expression. Related issues, such as child pornography, and the relationship between pornography and violence are also discussed.

Further, this Almanac sets forth the tools available to parents who are concerned about the availability of harmful subject matter in the media, including program blocking devices, and ratings systems developed by the motion picture, television, music, and videogame industries. In addition, the regulation of broadcast media by the Federal Communications Commission (FCC) is also discussed.

The advent of the computer age has presented new and novel issues to be addressed, as it is a difficult medium to monitor and control. This Almanac discusses the status of the current law, including the most recent legislation affecting materials available through the Internet and various on-line services, and the government's attempt to restrict material that is harmful to minors.

The Appendix provides resource directories, applicable statutes, and other pertinent information and data. The Glossary contains definitions of many of the terms used throughout the Almanac.

CHAPTER 1:
AN OVERVIEW OF OBSCENITY LAW

IN GENERAL

Throughout history, courts have struggled to define pornography and obscenity. The term "pornography" has generally been used to describe sexually explicit material. The term "obscenity" refers to the legal definition of whether such materials are protected under the First Amendment guarantees of free speech and free press.

Material that is deemed obscene is not constitutionally protected. However, the definition of obscenity has been narrowly construed. In general, to be considered obscene, the material must: (1) appeal to the prurient interest; (2) be patently offensive to the average person in society; and (3) lack serious value.

Many believe that First Amendment freedoms are presently under attack by the government as it seeks to regulate the Internet, music lyrics, and other forms of art and entertainment that are viewed as predominant factors in the "downfall" of morals and the increase in youth violence in the United States. They argue that the very purpose of the First Amendment is to protect the most controversial forms of expression from such government suppression and regulation. Their opponents argue that the framers of the Constitution were intent on protecting political speech, not every form of explicit or offensive expression now claiming constitutional protection.

Nevertheless, as discussed below, the simple language of the First Amendment leaves much to interpretation. Thus the United States Supreme Court has been called on to set standards and guidelines to resolve these disputes and determine whether particular forms of expression are obscene.

The Court has attempted to formulate certain tests to make this determination, usually basing their decision on contemporary moral standards.

However, a major problem exists in that what one person may deem "pornographic," another may perceive as "artistic expression."

THE FIRST AMENDMENT

The First Amendment to the United States Constitution provides that:

> Congress shall make no law respecting an establishment of religion, or prohibiting the free exercise thereof; or abridging the *freedom of speech*, or of the press, or the right of the people peaceably to assemble, and to petition the Government for a redress of grievances.

The First Amendment has been cited as the "protector" of free speech forbidding, among other things, government censorship. Not all speech, however, is protected. For example, material that is deemed "obscene" is not afforded protection under the First Amendment.

When considering "free speech" rights, the question is often asked: "What would the founding fathers think?" Considering the language and images that have infiltrated the arts and entertainment world in the late 20th century, it is unlikely that the materials currently deemed permissible would have ever been afforded constitutional protection in 1791 when the amendment was ratified. In fact, it is more likely that the publishers would be jailed.

Modern-day judicial decisions on a number of free speech issues, particularly those surrounding obscenity, simply would not have been contemplated by the original drafters. However, it has been held that the constitution is subject to interpretation as it relates to the times during which we live.

Content-Based Restrictions on Speech

The government adopts and enforces many measures that are designed to further a valid interest but which may have restrictive effects upon freedom of expression. In general, however, the government may not regulate speech because of its message, its ideas, its subject matter, or its content.

Most content-based restrictions on speech are struck down as unconstitutional. Such restrictions require: (1) a compelling governmental interest and; (2) a statute that is narrowly drawn to be upheld. Over the years, the Supreme Court has developed certain general constitutional standards or tests that are applicable to the First Amendment, including the following:

Vagueness

The "vagueness" doctrine generally requires that a law be precise enough to give fair warning to individuals that certain conduct is criminal, and provide adequate standards to enforcement agencies, fact finders, and reviewing courts. If the law does not give clear notice of what is prohibited, it violates due process.

Although this provision is applicable to any criminal and many civil statutes, it applies to the First Amendment because it is also concerned that protected conduct will be deterred out of fear that a particular law may apply. In fact, vagueness has been the basis for voiding a number of statutes, including obscenity laws, public demonstration prohibitions, and loyalty oath requirements.

Overbroad

If a law burdens more speech than is necessary for a compelling interest, it violates the First Amendment. Because there is a need for precision in drafting any law that affects First Amendment rights, any statute that is "overbroad," encompassing protected and unprotected speech and conduct, will generally be struck down as unconstitutional. In resolving a non-First Amendment issue, the Court may simply void the statute's application to the protected speech and/or conduct.

Least Restrictive Means

The Supreme Court has held that when a government endeavors to carry out a particular goal, and it has a variety of means to reach that goal, the government must use the measure that least interferes with an individual's First Amendment Rights. This is generally known as using the "least restrictive means necessary." In addition, the chosen measure must relate to achievement of the goal in order to be justified.

HISTORY OF EARLY CENSORSHIP LAWS

In this country, significant state and federal government intervention in the area of censorship of obscene materials did not occur until the mid to late 1800s. Prior to that time, there were some state laws criminalizing obscenity, but only sporadic convictions were obtained.

The *Hicklin* Test

Under the English common law, the rule for judging obscenity was formulated by Justice Cockburn in *Regina v. Hicklin*, L.R.3 Q.B. 360 (1868):

> [T]he test of obscenity is whether the tendency of the matter charged as obscenity is to deprave and corrupt those whose minds are open to such immoral influences, and into whose hands a publication of this sort may fall.

The *Hicklin* court apparently made its decision based on the content of isolated passages of the book rather than as a whole. The court enunciated two issues: (1) isolated passages; and (2) the susceptible person, which were paramount in the court's decision making, and formed the basis for the so-called *Hicklin* test.

The *Hicklin* test became the guiding principle for American courts through the early twentieth century.

The Anti-Obscenity Act of 1873 (The "Comstock Act")

In the mid-19th century, a censorship movement began to block so-called "indecent literature." The movement was spearheaded by a Connecticut man named Anthony Comstock. Comstock was responsible for organizing the New York Society for Suppression of Vice which, under New York law, was empowered with the rights to search, seize, and arrest.

Under The Anti-Obscenity Act of 1873, also known as the "Comstock Act," all material found to be "lewd," "indecent," "filthy," or "obscene," was banned. Following this lead, a number of other similar organizations sprung up across the country.

During the *Comstock* era, many books were banned and thousands of people were arrested. Books by such literary greats as Chaucer, Hemingway, Steinbeck, F. Scott Fitzgerald, and D.H. Lawrence, to name a few, were banned at one time or another under obscenity laws.

In addition, a federal law entitled the "Comstock Law," was passed which forbid sending obscene materials through the mail. A number of prosecutions were undertaken under this law.

The Anti-Obscenity Act was codified in the U.S. Code as follows:

Mailing obscene or crime-inciting matter (18 U.S.C. § 1461)

Every obscene, lewd, lascivious, indecent, filthy or vile article, matter, thing, device, or substance; and—

Every article or thing designed, adapted, or intended for producing abortion, or for any indecent or immoral use; and

Every article, instrument, substance, drug, medicine, or thing which is advertised or described in a manner calculated to lead another to use or apply it for producing abortion, or for any indecent or immoral purpose; and

Every written or printed card, letter, circular, book, pamphlet, advertisement, or notice of any kind giving information, directly or indirectly, where, or how, or from whom, or by what means any of such mentioned matters, articles, or things may be obtained or made, or where or by whom any act or operation of any kind for the procuring or producing of abortion will be done or performed, or how or by what means abortion may be produced, whether sealed or unsealed; and

Every paper, writing, advertisement, or representation that any article, instrument, substance, drug, medicine, or thing may, or can, be used or applied for producing abortion, or for any indecent or immoral purpose; and

Every description calculated to induce or incite a person to so use or apply any such article, instrument, substance, drug, medicine, or thing—

Is declared to be nonmailable matter and shall not be conveyed in the mails or delivered from any post office or by any letter carrier.

Whoever knowingly uses the mails for the mailing, carriage in the mails, or delivery of anything declared by this section or section 3001(e) of title 39 to be nonmailable, or knowingly causes to be delivered by mail according to the direction thereon, or at the place at which it is directed to be delivered by the person to whom it is addressed, or knowingly takes any such thing from the mails for the purpose of circulating or disposing thereof, or of aiding in the circulation or disposition thereof, shall be fined under this title or imprisoned not more than five years, or both, for the first such offense, and shall be fined under this title or imprisoned not more than ten years, or both, for each such offense thereafter.

The term "indecent," as used in this section includes matter of a character tending to incite arson, murder, or assassination.

THE DEMISE OF THE HICKLIN TEST

Through the early twentieth century, American courts applied the standard of obscenity articulated by the English court in the *Hicklin* case. However, as the 20th century progressed, censorship began to fall into disfavor, and the judiciary was called upon to set a clear path.

United States v. One Book Entitled Ulysses by James Joyce

In 1933, the *Hicklin* test met its final demise. In *United States v. One Book Entitled Ulysses by James Joyce*, 5 F.Supp. 182 (S.D.N.Y. 1933), Judge John Woolsey issued a landmark decision finding that the book *Ulysses* by James Joyce was not obscene.

Judge Woolsey rejected the "isolated passages" and the "susceptible person" doctrines, and opined that obscenity is to be judged by the effect of the book in its entirety (the "dominant effect"). Judge Woolsey also stated that the book "must be tested by the Court's opinion as to its effect on a person with average sex instincts . . . who plays . . . the same role . . . as does the *reasonable man* in the law of torts."

Judge Woolsey's decision in the *Ulysses* case was a significant shift in the policies of U.S. courts and legislatures towards obscenity. Before the *Ulysses* decision, it was largely held that laws prohibiting obscenity were not in conflict with the First Amendment.

The government appealed Judge Woolsey's decision to the Circuit Court of Appeals; however, Judge Learned Hand and Judge Augustus Hand affirmed the judgment.

SETTING A NEW STANDARD

Roth v. United States

In *Roth v. United States*, 354 U.S. 476 (1957), the U.S. Supreme Court upheld the constitutionality of the federal Anti-Obscenity Act of 1873, and the conviction of Mr. Samuel Roth, a New York publisher and seller of books and magazines.

In addition, the Court expressly held that the *Hicklin* test was an unconstitutional restriction of the freedoms of speech and the press, and replaced it with a new standard similar to that enunciated by Judge Woolsey in *Ulysses*. The new obscenity test focused on "whether to the *average person*, applying contemporary community standards, the dominant theme of the material *taken as a whole* appeals to the prurient interest."

The Court further ruled that although ideas having even the slightest redeeming social importance are protected, obscenity is not constitutionally protected under the First and Fourteenth Amendments because it "utterly lacks any redeeming social importance."

THE VALUE TEST

Jacobellis v. State of Ohio

In *Jacobellis v. State of Ohio*, 378 U.S. 184 (1964), the U.S. Supreme Court reversed the conviction of Mr. Jacobellis, an Ohio theater manager. Mr. Jacobellis had been convicted of violating a state statute that prohibited the showing of obscene films.

The majority opinion expanded on the *Roth* test by holding that materials which *have literary, scientific or artistic value*, or are of *social importance*, or *advocate ideas*, are constitutionally protected even if they involve sexual matter.

Further, the Court stated that to be obscene, the material must be "utterly without redeeming social importance." Although Justice Brennan had used this language in the *Roth* decision, it was not made a part of the obscenity test until *Jacobellis*.

Despite the Supreme Court's attempt *in* Jacobellis to devise a test, defining obscenity is still a difficult task. In that regard, a statement made by Justice Potter Stewart in that case is often quoted: "I know it when I see it."

REFINING THE ROTH STANDARD

Memoirs v. Massachusetts

In *Memoirs v. Massachusetts*, 383 U.S. 413 (1966), the United States Supreme Court refined the test of obscenity and set forth three elements which must be established:

In *A Book Named "John Cleland's Memoirs of a Woman of Pleasure" v. Massachusetts*, 383 U.S. 413 (1966)), the U.S. Supreme Court refined the test of obscenity and set forth the three elements that must be established to determine obscenity:

1. the dominant theme of the material taken as a whole appeals to prurient interest in sex (the "Roth" standard);

2. the material is patently offensive because it affronts contemporary community standards relating to the description or representation of sexual matters; and

3. the material is utterly without redeeming social value.

A LANDMARK DECISION

Miller v. California

In 1973, the United States Supreme Court made sweeping changes in the obscenity test, and abandoned the requirement that the material be "utterly without redeeming social value."

As set forth in the majority decision in *Miller v. California*, 413 U.S. 15 (1973), the Court held that the test of obscenity would be determined by the following three-part test:

1. Prurient Interest—whether the average person, applying contemporary community standards, would find that the work, taken as a whole, appeals to the prurient interest;

2. Patently Offensive—whether the work depicts or describes, in a patently offensive way, sexual conduct specifically defined by the applicable state law; and

3. Value—whether the work, taken as a whole, lacks serious literary, artistic, political, or scientific value.

Thus if the work (1) appeals to the prurient interest; and (2) is patently offensive, then in order to be constitutionally protected, the Court held that it must meet the third prong, i.e., it must contain serious literary, artistic, political, or scientific value.

The first two prongs of the *Miller* test concern issues of fact that are generally decided by a jury applying "contemporary community standards" as its measuring stick. However, the definition of "community" is much broader than one's "neighborhood." For example, in New York, the "community" has been held to refer to the entire State of New York.

Examples of Prohibited Behavior

The Court set forth some permissible examples of prohibited behavior to guide states in formulating their obscenity statutes, as follows:

1. Patently offensive representations or descriptions of ultimate sexual acts, normal or perverted, actual or simulated.

2. Patently offensive representations or descriptions of masturbation, excretory functions, and lewd exhibition of the genitals.

The text of *Miller v. California* can be found in Appendix 1, "Miller v. California [413 U.S. 15 (1973)]," of this Almanac.

Pope v. Illinois—The Reasonable Person Standard

In *Pope v. Illinois*, 481 U.S. 497 (1987), the U.S. Supreme Court evaluated the "average person" standard as it applied to the third prong of the *Miller* test. The Court redefined the part of the test concerning the literary, artistic, political, or scientific value of the material, holding that the standard would now be measured by whether "a reasonable person" would find such value in the material, taken as a whole.

The text of *Pope v. Miller* can be found in Appendix 2, "Pope v. Illinois [381 U.S. 497 (1987)]," of this Almanac.

PRIVACY OF THE HOME

Stanley v. Georgia

In *Stanley v. Georgia*, 394 U.S. 557 (1969), the U.S. Supreme Court reversed the conviction of Mr. Stanley, and struck down a Georgia statute which made it illegal for a person to possess obscene matter in the privacy of one's own home.

CENSORSHIP IN THE ARTS AND MEDIA

Artistic freedom is protected under the First Amendment, and has been interpreted by the Supreme Court to include a broad spectrum of artistic expression, including books, paintings, music, sculptures, theater, movies, television, and magazines, etc.

When the Supreme Court is called upon to determine whether there has been an infringement on artistic expression, they generally conduct a two-part analysis: (1) there can be no censorship or restriction on artistic expression merely because the content offends the listener, even if that viewpoint is shared by the majority; and (2) artistic expression may be restricted if it will cause clear *direct and imminent harm* to an important societal interest.

Sexual expression in the areas of entertainment and the media has always been a target by groups wishing to censor the content of music lyrics, television programming, movies, and the theater. Proponents of censorship argue that violence and immorality among the nation's youth correlates with the language and images children are exposed to through the media. They take the position that murder, violence, and explicit sexual images portrayed in the media should not be protected, as they often offend religious beliefs, degrade women, and endanger children.

Opponents of censorship argue that there is no evidence that fictional violence causes otherwise balanced people to become violent. They take the position that a free society is based on the principle that each and every individual has the right to decide the type of entertainment he or she wants to accept or reject, and that the Government has no right to make that decision. They suggest that those who may be offended by violence or sexual images should merely refrain from watching a particular movie or television program, and concerned parents can prevent access to certain programming through the use of available blocking devices.

It is true that protection of the First Amendment right of freedom of expression in America has been fervently protected over the years. Nevertheless, the framers of the Constitution could not have imagined television, movies, and the Internet, and the type of provocative and controversial images and ideas that they exhibit.

The U.S. Supreme Court has consistently upheld the right to freedom of expression, and has held that indecent expression is entitled to some degree of constitutional protection. Nevertheless, the Court has also recognized that indecency and profanity in some media must be regulated.

Regulation of broadcast media is discussed more fully in Chapter 5, "FCC Regulation of Broadcast Media," of this Almanac.

Several of the most significant censorship rulings involving the arts are set forth below.

Magazine Publications

In 1942, the U.S. Post Office began denying second-class special mailing privileges to publications it deemed immoral or which did not contribute to the public good. Of course, this resulted in a large increase in mailing costs for the publishers.

After its second class mailing permit was revoked, *Esquire Magazine* challenged this Post Office regulation in the U.S. District Court, where it lost. The ruling was appealed to the U.S. Court of Appeals for the D.C. Circuit, which reversed the lower court ruling.

The case was then appealed to the U.S. Supreme Court, which affirmed the Court of Appeals decision, holding that restrictions on second-class mail rates cannot be based on a Post Office determination that certain publications do not "contribute to the public good."

The Motion Picture Industry

In the early 1900s, the U.S. Supreme Court held that the First Amendment did not apply to the motion picture industry because it was a business. This ruling led to intense censorship of motion pictures.

The Supreme Court changed its position in 1952 under its ruling in the case of *Burstyn v. Wilson*, 343 U.S. 495 (1952). The *Burstyn* case involved a movie entitled *The Miracle*, which was met with intense criticism by religious groups. The film was subsequently banned in New York.

On appeal, the Supreme Court held that the First and Fourteenth Amendment protections were not forfeited simply because a movie is made for profit, although the obscenity test remained applicable. Underlying the Court's change in position was its reasoning that motion pictures, like literary materials, were an important medium for the communication of political and social ideas.

Theatrical Productions

The most significant decision concerning censorship and the theater involved the rock musical *Hair*. The road company was barred from performing in a city-leased theater in Chattanooga, Tennessee because the directors of the theater board deemed the production obscene. The promoter of the production, Southeastern Promotions, Ltd., filed suit (*Southeastern Promotions, Ltd. v. Steve Conrad*, 95 S. Ct. 1239 (1975)).

Following a hearing before the U.S. District Court, the jury: (1) concurred that the production was obscene; and (2) found that the group nudity and simulated sex acts were not speech, and thus not protected under the First Amendment.

In 1975, the U.S. Supreme Court, on appeal, reversed the District Court's ruling without making a determination on whether or not the production was obscene. Instead, the Court found that the board's action in denying use of the theater constituted a system of *prior restraint* that violated the First Amendment.

The Court concluded that the burden of proving that the material was unprotected rested on the censor, i.e., the board, and the board was responsible for initiating the judicial proceedings. The Court also pointed out that "any restraint prior to judicial review can be imposed only for a specified brief period, for the purpose of preserving the status quo," and that "prompt judicial determination must be assured."

THE CRIME OF OBSCENITY—NEW YORK PENAL CODE

An examination of the crime of obscenity under the New York Penal Code is set forth in this section as a representative state statutory scheme that complies with the constitutional requirements of the First Amendment.

Obscenity Defined

Obscenity is defined in § 235.00 of the New York Penal Code as follows:

1. Obscene—Any material or performance is "obscene" if:

    (a) the average person, applying contemporary community standards, would find that considered as a whole, its predominant appeal is to the prurient interest in sex; and

    (b) it depicts or describes in a patently offensive manner, actual or simulated: sexual intercourse, sodomy, sexual bestiality, masturbation, sadism, masochism, excretion, or lewd exhibition of the genitals; and

    (c) considered as a whole, it lacks serious literary, artistic, political, and scientific value.

Predominant appeal shall be judged with reference to ordinary adults unless it appears from the character of the material or the circumstances of its dissemination to be designed for children or another specially susceptible audience.

The Degree of Crime

Obscenity was originally a single degree crime under New York law. The crime was later divided into three distinct degrees of offense, the most basic of which is obscenity in the third degree.

Obscenity in the Third Degree—New York Penal Code § 235.05

Obscenity in the third degree contains two subdivisions:

Obscene Material

The first part of the statute governs those defendants who "promote, or possess with intent to promote, any obscene material." Material is defined as anything tangible that is capable of being used or adapted to arouse interest, whether through the medium of reading, observation, sound, or in any other manner.

Simple possession of obscene material is not prohibited under the statute. Nevertheless, if an individual possesses six or more identical or similar obscene articles, he or she is presumed to possess them with intent to promote them.

Obscene Performance

The second part refers to those who "produce, present or direct an obscene performance or participate in a portion thereof which is obscene or which contributes to its obscenity." Performance is defined as any play, motion picture, dance, or other exhibition performed before an audience. Both the promoter of the obscene performance, and the participant, may be prosecuted under this section.

Obscenity in the third degree is a class A misdemeanor.

Obscenity in the Second Degree—New York Penal Code § 235.06

A person is guilty of obscenity in the second degree when he commits the crime of obscenity in the third degree as set forth above, after having been previously convicted of obscenity in the third degree.

Obscenity in the second degree is a class E felony.

Obscenity in the First Degree—New York Penal Code § 235.07

A person is guilty of obscenity in the first degree when, knowing its content and character, he wholesale promotes or possesses with intent to wholesale promote, any obscene material.

"Wholesale promote" is defined as manufacturing, issuing, selling, providing, mailing, delivering, transferring, transmuting, publishing, distributing, circulating, disseminating, or offering or agreeing to do the same for purposes of resale. The purpose of this provision is to more strictly punish those who mass produce and distribute obscenity.

Obscenity in the first degree is a class D felony.

Required Mental State

The New York statute requires that the defendant know that the content and the character of the material or performance is obscene.

In *People v. Finkelstein*, 9 NY2d 342 (1961), the New York Court of Appeals held that only those who are *aware* of the obscene character of the material or performance should be punished because it is the *intentional* promotion of obscene materials that the statute seeks to ban.

Nevertheless, possession of obscene materials has been held to permit an inference that the possessor is aware of the content and character of the materials (*People v. Reisman*, 29 NY2d 278 (1971)).

The New York statute also states that intent may be presumed under the following circumstances:

Obscenity; Presumptions—New York Penal Code § 235.10

1. A person who promotes or wholesale promotes obscene material, or possesses the same with intent to promote or wholesale promote it, in the course of his business is presumed to do so with knowledge of its content and character.

2. A person who possesses six or more identical or similar obscene articles is presumed to possess them with intent to promote the same.

Affirmative Defenses

The New York Penal Code sets forth two affirmative defenses to the crime of obscenity:

Justified Purpose

The first affirmative defense applies to persons or institutions that have some scientific, educational, or governmental purpose for possessing or viewing obscene materials.

Motion Picture Theater Employees

The second affirmative defense applies to certain employees of a motion picture theater who (1) are in a nonsupervisory position; and (2) have no financial interest in promotion or presentation of the obscene material or performance.

SALE OR DISTRIBUTION OF OBSCENE MATERIAL TO MINORS

Sexual content has traditionally been at the core of censorship debates. However, the First Amendment has since extended somewhat of a blanket protection over sexual materials directed towards adults.

Nevertheless, censorship disputes continue to arise when children are exposed to materials and information involving sex, and the concern is inevitably raised that such exposure is "harmful" to a child. As set forth below, a number of statutes have been enacted to protect children from obscene material, and such statutes have been upheld as constitutional.

Ginsberg v. New York

Five years before the *Miller* test was established, as discussed above, the U.S. Supreme Court formulated a different standard concerning access to sexual material by minors.

In *Ginsberg v. State of New York*, 390 U.S. 629 (1968), the U.S. Supreme Court affirmed the conviction of Samuel Ginsberg for violation of a New York statute that prohibited the sale of obscene material to minors under the age of 17.

In upholding the conviction, the Court upheld a New York statute that criminalized the distribution of material deemed "harmful to minors" without a showing of actual harm or a compelling state interest. The Court ruled:

> [T]he concept of obscenity . . . may vary according to the group to whom the questionable material is directed. . . Because of the State's exigent interest in preventing distribution to children of objectionable material, it can exercise its power to protect the health, safety, welfare and morals of its community by barring the distribution to children of books recognized to be suitable for adults.

The Court deferred to the state legislature's determination that exposure to such material was harmful to minors, and found this to be a rational reason for enacting the statute. Thus material that appeals to the "prurient, shameful or morbid" interest of minors; lacks serious social value for minors; and is "patently offensive" based on adult views of what is fit for minors, may be deemed "harmful to minors."

The New York Statute

The New York statute prohibiting the dissemination of indecent material to a minor provides:

Disseminating Indecent Material to Minors in the Second Degree— New York Penal Code § 235.21

A person is guilty of disseminating indecent material to minors in the second degree when:

1. With knowledge of its character and content, he sells or loans to a minor for monetary consideration:

(a) Any picture, photograph, drawing, sculpture, motion picture film, or similar visual representation or image of a person or portion of the human body which depicts nudity, sexual conduct or sado-masochistic abuse and which is harmful to minors; or

(b) Any book, pamphlet, magazine, printed matter however reproduced, or sound recording which contains any matter enumerated in paragraph (a) hereof, or explicit and detailed verbal descriptions or narrative account of sexual excitement, sexual conduct or sado-masochistic abuse and which taken as a whole, is harmful to minors; or

2. Knowing the character and content of a motion picture, show or other presentation which, in whole or in part, depicts nudity, sexual conduct or sado-masochistic abuse, and which is harmful to minors, he:

(a) Exhibits such motion picture, show or other presentation to a minor for a monetary consideration; or

(b) Sells to a minor an admission ticket or pass to premises whereon there is exhibited or to be exhibited such motion picture, show or other presentation; or

(c) Admits a minor for a monetary consideration to premises whereon there is exhibited or to be exhibited such motion picture show or other presentation; or

3. Knowing the character and content of the communication which, in whole or in part, depicts actual or simulated nudity, sexual conduct or sado-masochistic abuse, and which is harmful to minors, he intentionally uses any computer communication system allowing the input, output, examination or transfer, of computer data or computer programs from one computer to another, to initiate or engage in such communication with a person who is a minor.

Disseminating indecent material to minors in the second degree is a class E felony.

Disseminating Indecent Material to Minors in the First degree— New York Penal Code § 235.22

A person is guilty of disseminating indecent material to minors in the first degree when:

1. Knowing the character and content of the communication which, in whole or in part, depicts or describes, either in words or images actual or simulated nudity, sexual conduct or sado-masochistic abuse, and which is harmful to minors, he intentionally uses any computer communication system allowing the input, output, examination or transfer, of computer data or computer programs from one

computer to another, to initiate or engage in such communication with a person who is a minor; and

2. By means of such communication he importunes, invites or induces a minor to engage in sexual intercourse, oral sexual conduct or anal sexual conduct, or sexual contact with him, or to engage in a sexual performance, obscene sexual performance, or sexual conduct for his benefit.

Disseminating indecent material to minors in the first degree is a class D felony.

Federal Law

Federal law prohibits a person from using the mail, or any of the means of interstate commerce, including a computer, to knowingly transfer obscene materials to someone the person knows is under 16 years of age. The statute reads as follows:

Transfer of Obscene Material to Minors (18 U.S.C. § 1470)

Whoever using the mail or any facility or means of interstate or foreign commerce, knowingly transfers obscene matter to another individual who has not attained the age of 16 years, knowing that such other individual has not attained the age of 16 years, or attempts to do so, shall be fined under this title, imprisoned not more than 10 years, or both.

For example, it would be a crime to knowingly email an obscene picture to a 15 year-old.

As further discussed in Chapter 2, "Obscenity and the Internet," of this Almanac, there are three other statutes designed to protect children using the Internet.

1. It is illegal to knowingly use an interactive computer service to display obscenity or child pornography in a manner that makes it available to a person under 18 (47 U.S.C. § 223(d)).

2. It is illegal to knowingly making a commercial communication via the Internet that includes obscenity and is available to any minor under age 17 (47 U.S.C. § 231).

3. It is illegal to use Internet domain names with the intent to mislead a minor into viewing material that is harmful to minors, or mislead any person into viewing obscenity (18 U.S.C. § 2252B).

INTERNATIONAL OBSCENITY LAWS

As discussed above, the definition of obscenity in the United States has evolved throughout history, as the Supreme Court has struggled to come up with a test that balances constitutional considerations with the changing morals of American society. However, because the definition of obscenity largely depends on prevailing societal and cultural norms, material that may be acceptable in one country may be entirely prohibited in another.

As a result of these cultural differences, the laws that govern obscenity, pornography, and indecency, vary greatly among countries. In some countries, pornography is legal whereas in other countries, the punishment for those who violate these prohibitions includes the death penalty.

For example, in 1968, Denmark became the first country in the world to legalize pornography, whereas in Egypt, pornography is completely illegal. Many countries have restrictions on access to pornographic materials, however, actual enforcement is lax and punishment is nonexistent. Nevertheless, child pornography is generally illegal in all countries.

In countries that view pornography as an abomination against religion, punishment is severe. For example, in 2008, owners of Arabic television were warned that the airing of "immodest" shows, particularly during the holy month of Ramadan, would result in execution under Saudi Arabia's Islamic Sharia law.

The People's Republic of China has also imposed strict laws against indecency. In 2002, Internet pornography was outlawed, and all Web sites were required to remove pornographic material. In 2008, a total ban on the production of pornographic movies was instituted.

CHAPTER 2:
OBSCENITY AND THE INTERNET

IN GENERAL

Regulating indecent material on the Internet and various other online services has become a challenging task. There is much concern over how to prevent a child from accessing sexually explicit materials and participating in sexually-related discussions through their computers, and still protect the First Amendment rights of adults to engage in constitutionally protected indecent speech.

Presently, there are no universally accepted laws that regulate the availability of Internet pornography. Each country is free to develop its own law in this regard. Thus what is perfectly legal in one country may be deemed criminal in another country. For example, Saudi Arabia restricts the availability of pornographic Web sites by mandating Internet filters, and assessing stiff penalties to violators.

The U.S. Congress has attempted to address this problem by passing legislation, which is further discussed below. However, litigation concerning these efforts to regulate speech on the Internet has been largely unsuccessful, as U.S. Courts have routinely held that Internet communication is entitled to the full measure of First Amendment protection.

Many staunch First Amendment supporters contend that there should be no restrictions on adult access, and state that there is no need for federal laws regulating information that may be broadcast in "cyberspace." They argue that offensive images do not merely project themselves onto the screen, but must be sought out by the subscriber.

They believe that the burden of restricting child access should be placed upon parents and legal guardians who can use existing technology to prevent their children from accessing Internet sites which exhibit sexually explicit material. In practice, however, this is difficult, particularly since many children in this technological society are far more computer literate than their parents.

LEGAL STATUS

The legal status of obscenity and pornography on the Internet in the United States is quite unsettled. As discussed below, legislators have attempted to enact legislation to regulate content, but these laws have been challenged and struck down. It is, however, well-settled that online child pornography is illegal.

As discussed in Chapter 1, "An Overview of Obscenity Law," of this Almanac, the test currently used to determine whether material is obscene was articulated in *Miller v. California*, 413 U.S. 15 (1973), and uses "contemporary community standards" as the measuring stick. Thus if the "community" determines that a particular work is obscene, it is illegal. Thus a book that is deemed obscene and therefore banned in rural Montana is not necessarily illegal in New York if the "community" does not find it obscene.

The problem lies in deciding which community's standards would make the obscenity determination. Thus the Court has been unable to apply the *Miller* test to determine whether material on the Internet is obscene. Which community standard would apply? Will the most restrictive local standards of obscenity in the country govern or will the Court fashion a standard that applies only to the Internet?

The Court is attempting to resolve this difficult issue. In the meantime, it is nearly impossible to restrict access to obscene material on the Internet to any minor who has access to a computer and the Internet. Most Web sites that offer material intended for adults have instituted measures to try and prevent access by minors, however, it is easy for a child to get around these measures if he or she is intent on doing so.

For example, an adult-oriented Web site may contain a warning when the user accesses the site, and require the user to click on a box that states he or she is over the age of 18. The minor simply clicks that box and has immediate access. Some Web sites go a little further and require registration with a credit card before the user is granted access. Since most minors do not have a credit card, this requirement serves as a method of age verification.

THE COMMUNICATIONS DECENCY ACT OF 1996

The first attempt at regulating indecency on the Internet was the Communications Decency Act (CDA), signed into law by President Clinton on February 8, 1996. The CDA banned the "knowing" transmission of obscene materials to minors via broadcast media, including the Internet. The CDA also prohibited the publication of certain sexual material that were deemed patently offensive according to contemporary community standards, unless those materials were protected from access by minors. Violations of the Act carried criminal penalties that included prison and hefty fines.

Reno v. American Civil Liberties Union

In drafting the CDA, lawmakers expected there to be immediate constitutional challenges. Therefore, they included provisions in the law expediting review by the U.S. Supreme Court. Special panels of federal judges were designated to hear the challenges first and the decision of the panel could then be appealed directly to the Supreme Court.

Lawmakers were correct in their prediction because a number of organizations, spearheaded by the American Civil Liberties Union (ACLU), immediately filed a lawsuit challenging the constitutionality of the CDA. The ACLU argued that the CDA constituted government censorship and the establishment of new speech crimes for the Internet and online communications. They also argued that the CDA failed to use the constitutionally required "least restrictive means" in regulating protected speech to obtain its goal, and invaded the privacy rights of persons communicating online.

On June 12, 1996, the United States District Court for the Eastern District of Pennsylvania ruled that the CDA was unconstitutional on its face. The Court held that portions of the CDA were too vague as well as too broad. The Justice Department filed an appeal of this ruling to the U.S. Supreme Court.

In 1997, the U.S. Supreme Court heard the appeal in *Reno v. ACLU*, 521 U.S. 844 (1997), and issued its landmark decision, holding that the "indecent transmission" and "patently offensive" provisions of the law violated the free speech guarantees of the First Amendment.

According to the Court, the CDA imposed an unconstitutional censorship scheme on the Internet, described by a federal judge as "the most participatory form of mass speech yet developed." The ruling basically gave the Internet the same protection accorded books and other printed materials.

THE CHILD ONLINE PROTECTION ACT OF 1998

In response to the *Reno* ruling, Congress enacted the Child Online Protection Act (COPA) in October 1998. The Act was dubbed the "CDA II"—as successor to the invalidated CDA. President Clinton signed the bill, notwithstanding the fact that the Department of Justice expressed reservations about its constitutionality.

American Civil Liberties Union v. Reno II

Almost immediately following its passage, the Act was challenged on the ground that it violated the First Amendment, as applied by the Supreme Court in the *Reno* case. The ACLU represented a number of plaintiffs who publish materials online, including an art gallery, Salon. com magazine, Powell's Bookstore, and the producer of a Web site providing information on sexuality to disabled people.

Under COPA, all *commercial* distributors of *material harmful to minors* were required to protect their sites from access by minors, defined as children under the age of 17. "Material harmful to minors" was defined as materials that by "contemporary community standards" were judged to appeal to the "prurient interest," and that showed sexual acts or nudity.

An affirmative defense under the Act was that the Web site: (1) required the use of a credit card, debit account, adult access code, or adult personal identification number; (2) accepted a digital certificate that verifies age; or (3) used other reasonable age verification measures.

In 1998, an injunction blocking the federal government from enforcing COPA was obtained. The case continued to work its way through the courts for another ten years, through several administrations, as the parties took turns appealing unfavorable decisions.

In 1999, the U.S. Court of Appeals for the Third Circuit upheld the injunction and struck down the law. The Court ruled that using "community standards" as part of the definition of "harmful materials" was too broad.

In 2002, the U.S. Supreme Court reviewed the lower court's ruling, and found that its reasoning for striking down the law was insufficient. In an 8–1 ruling, the Court held that using community standards to determine what online material is harmful to minors did not violate the First Amendment. The case was returned to the Circuit Court which, in 2003, again struck down the law as unconstitutional because it hindered free speech among adults.

Ashcroft v. American Civil Liberties Union

An appeal followed and, in 2004, the Supreme Court upheld the injunction as unconstitutional in *Ashcroft v. American Civil Liberties Union*, 542 U.S. 656 (2004). However, the case was returned to the lower court to determine whether there were newer technical developments that could resolve the issue.

In March 2007, the U.S. District Court for the Eastern District held that COPA was an unconstitutional violation of the First and Fifth Amendments.

American Civil Liberties Union v. Mukasey

In July 2008, the government appealed, and the U.S. Court of Appeals for the Third Circuit upheld the ban on COPA. The Court again affirmed that COPA was unconstitutional because it was not tailored to advance the government's interest in protecting children.

The Court also held that there are less restrictive, equally effective alternatives to COPA, and that COPA was unconstitutionally overbroad and vague. In its ruling, the Court stated that COPA, like the CDA before it, "effectively suppresses a large amount of speech that adults have a constitutional right to receive and to address to one another."

THE CHILDREN'S INTERNET PROTECTION ACT OF 2000

In 2000, Congress passed the Children's Internet Protection Act (CIPA), another law intended to protect children from access to Internet pornography. CIPA required that schools and public libraries use filtering software on all public computers to prevent users from viewing images deemed "harmful to minors." Public libraries that did not comply with the law would not be eligible for federal subsidies for Internet connectivity.

Filtering Software

Filtering software is designed to control the content of material available on a particular computer. For purposes of CIPA, filtering software is intended to prevent computer users from viewing images that are obscene or depict child pornography; to limit the Web sites children have access; and to restrict content deemed harmful to minors. However, librarians would be able to bypass the filtering software for adults who were undertaking legitimate research.

U.S. v. American Library Association

CIPA was challenged by the American Library Association (ALA), which claimed the law violated the First Amendment. The ALA argued that filtering software blocks an extensive amount of useful information because the software is unable to discriminate based on context. Therefore, important information concerning, e.g., sex education and health matters, would be filtered out regardless of its worth.

The ALA also argued that filtering software takes away individual choice, imposes filtering on everyone, and treats users of all ages identically, without allowing the consumer to determine what and why certain information may be unavailable. The lower court agreed to block enforcement of the law, and the government appealed the lower court decision.

In *U.S. v. American Library Association, Inc.*, 539 U.S. 194 (2003), the U.S. Supreme Court reversed the lower court ruling and held that the law was constitutional. The Supreme Court concluded that, as long as the librarian was able to unblock filtered material or disable the Internet software filter upon an adult user's request, "[T]he [government's] interest in protecting young library users from material inappropriate for minors is legitimate and even compelling, as all Members of the Court appear to agree."

Current Legal Status

Insofar as the U.S. Supreme Court upheld the constitutionality of the Children's Internet Protection Act (CIPA), the law is presently in force, unlike its predecessors, CDA and COPA, as discussed above.

CIPA Provisions

Internet Safety Policy

Under CIPA, schools and public libraries may not receive the discounts offered by the E-rate Internet connection program unless they certify that they have an Internet safety policy and technology protection measures in place. The Internet safety policy must include technology protection measures to block or filter Internet access to pictures that are: (1) obscene; (2) child pornography; or (3) harmful to minors.

Schools and libraries subject to CIPA must also certify that, as part of their Internet safety policy, they are educating minors about appropriate online behavior. This includes "cyberbullying" awareness and response, and interaction with other individuals on social networking sites and in chat rooms. In addition, schools are required to adopt and enforce a policy to monitor online activities of minors.

Neighborhood Children's Internet Protection Act

Section 1732 of CIPA sets forth additional Internet safety policy requirements for schools and libraries that address children's use of the Internet. Schools and libraries subject to CIPA must adopt and implement a policy addressing the following:

1. access by minors to inappropriate matter on the Internet;

2. the safety and security of minors when using electronic mail, chat rooms, and other forms of direct electronic communications;

3. unauthorized access, including so-called "hacking," and other unlawful activities by minors online;

4. unauthorized disclosure, use, and dissemination of personal information regarding minors; and

5. restricting minors' access to materials harmful to them.

Disabling Provision

As discussed above, the primary reason that CIPA withstood the constitutional attack against it by the American Library Association is because the law provides that an authorized person may disable the blocking or filtering measure during any use by an adult to enable access for bona fide research or other lawful purposes.

Expedited Judicial Review

Section 1741 of CIPA provides for expedited judicial review of the Act if there is a constitutional challenge. Under this provision, the challenge will first be heard by a district court of three judges. The decision of this three-judge panel is reviewable as a matter of right by direct appeal to the U.S. Supreme Court within 20 days of the lower court's ruling.

Selected provisions of the Children's Internet Protection Act can be found in Appendix 3, "Children's Internet Protection Act—Selected Provisions [Pub. L. No. 106-554, 12/21/2000]," of this Almanac.

PROTECTING YOUR CHILDREN IN CYBERSPACE

Society, government, and parents have a special interest in protecting the nation's children. We are acutely aware of the worldly dangers that confront children in their daily lives, and have taken many steps to ensure their safety from sexual predators, and restrict their access to pornographic materials.

One insidious form of danger has emerged in a format that is becoming increasingly difficult to monitor and regulate. The peril lies in the world of "cyberspace"—the Internet. Unfortunately, children are often more computer savvy than the parents who desire to protect them from these risks. However, the responsibility of safeguarding children must extend to cyberspace, as the consequences may be as damaging and injurious as anything a child may confront in the physical world.

The primary areas of risk to children online include: (1) the production and distribution of child pornography; (2) the online solicitation of children; and (3) exposure of obscene and pornographic images online that lead to psychological harm to children.

Production and Distribution of Child Pornography on the Internet

It is a violation of federal law to download child pornography from an Internet Web site. Even in cases where the image itself has not traveled in interstate or foreign commerce, federal law may still be violated if the materials used to create the image—e.g., the DVD on which the child pornography is stored—travels in interstate or foreign commerce.

Nevertheless, according to The National Center for Missing and Exploited Children (NCMEC), child pornography is a multi-billion dollar industry and among the fastest growing criminal segments on the Internet. According to the Federal Bureau of Investigation (FBI), child pornography revenue is estimated to be as high as twenty billion dollars per year.

In fact, child pornography accounts for approximately one-fifth of all Internet pornography. Digital and web cameras have made child pornography easy and inexpensive to produce and distribute over the Internet. It is estimated that 20% of all pornography available on the Internet involves children. ECPAT is an acronym that stands for "End Child Prostitution, Child Pornography and Trafficking of Children for Sexual Purposes."

According to statistics cited by NCMEC, since 1997, the number of child pornography images on the Internet is estimated to have increased by 1500%. According to a 2002 report by ECPAT International, a global network of organizations seeking to eliminate child pornography and related offenses, approximately 100,000 child pornography Web sites existed on the Internet in 2001.

In addition, the Congressionally-mandated Cyber-Tipline operated by NCMEC received 21,603 reports of child pornography in 2001, compared with 106,176 reports in 2004, accounting for a 491% increase over the four-year period.

Online Solicitation of Children

The Internet has evolved into a popular social environment for children. Many children e-mail, chat, video-chat, share music, and interact regularly online. They have online access with their cellphones, which they use to text each other, take pictures, and upload images and videos to the Internet. This manner of communication has become as common, if not more, than the days when teenagers spent a large portion of their free time talking on the telephone.

The growing concern is not so much the interaction among children, but the fact that adult predators have entered these chat rooms and befriended vulnerable children. Oftentimes, these predators will use images of child pornography as a means to desensitize these children, and lower their sexual inhibitions.

Child predators will try to entice a naïve child into taking sexually explicit photos or videos via a webcam or cellphone, and have the child upload the images or videos online. The child may not fully realize that those images may forever circulate the worldwide web without recourse.

These depraved individuals may also lure a vulnerable child into a face-to-face meeting, where the child is sexually assaulted or otherwise victimized. Sexual predators may use the child to produce pornographic images that are then distributed globally through Web sites where the images are traded among pedophiles.

According to EPCAT International, cyberspace is host to more than 1 million images of tens of thousands of children subjected to sexual abuse and exploitation.

Online Exposure to Pornography

In addition to the physical and emotional injuries suffered by children who are lured into the production of child pornography is the psychological harm to children who are exposed to pornographic images of both adults and children on the Internet. Some minors seek out this material, which is readily available online, without realizing the harm they may be inflicting upon themselves. Other children are involuntarily exposed to harmful images. And, as discussed above, early introduction to such graphic images can damage the normal course of a child's sexual orientation. This is a depraved method of inducting children into abnormal sexual behaviors and conditioning them to violent and degrading images.

FBI Warning Signs

The FBI has set forth a number of warning signs that may indicate a child may be accessing age-inappropriate and harmful material online or may be at risk for being victimized by a child sex offender:

1. Your child spends large amounts of time online, especially at night— Children online are at the greatest risk during the evening hours.

While offenders are online around the clock, most work during the day and spend their evenings online trying to locate and lure children or seeking pornography.

2. You find pornography on your child's computer—Pornography is often used in the sexual victimization of children. Sex offenders often supply their potential victims with pornography as a means of opening sexual discussions and for seduction. Child pornography may be used to show the child victim that sex between children and adults is "normal."

3. Your child receives phone calls from men you don't know or is making calls, sometimes long distance, to numbers you don't recognize—While talking to a child victim online is a thrill for a computer-sex offender, it can be very cumbersome. Most want to talk to the children on the telephone. They often engage in "phone sex" with the children and often seek to set up an actual meeting for real sex.

4. Your child receives mail, gifts, or packages from someone you don't know—As part of the seduction process, it is common for offenders to send letters, photographs, and all manner of gifts to their potential victims. Computer-sex offenders have even sent plane tickets in order for the child to travel across the country to meet them.

5. Your child turns the computer monitor off or quickly changes the screen on the monitor when you come into the room—A child looking at pornographic images or having sexually explicit conversations does not want you to see it on the screen.

6. Your child becomes withdrawn from the family—Computer-sex offenders will work very hard at driving a wedge between a child and their family or at exploiting their relationship. They will accentuate any minor problems at home that the child might have. Children may also become withdrawn after sexual victimization.

7. Your child is using an online account belonging to someone else—Even if you don't subscribe to an Internet service, your child may meet an offender while online at a friend's house or the library. Most computers come preloaded with Internet software. Computer-sex offenders will sometimes provide potential victims with a computer account for communications with them.

The FBI advises parents who suspect their child is accessing pornography online or communicating with a sexual predator online to review what is on the child's computer. Pornography or any kind of sexual communication can be a warning sign.

In addition, monitor the child's access to all types of live electronic communications, including chat rooms and instant messages, as well as the child's e-mail. Computer-sex offenders usually meet potential victims via chat rooms. After meeting a child online, they will continue to communicate electronically often via e-mail.

If any of the following scenarios occur via the Internet, the FBI and local or state enforcement agencies should be notified:

1. your child or anyone in the household has received child pornography;

2. your child has been sexually solicited by someone who knows that your child is under 18 years of age;

3. your child has received sexually explicit images from someone that knows your child is under the age of 18.

In the meantime, keep the computer turned off in order to preserve any evidence for future law enforcement use. Unless directed to do so by the law enforcement agency, you should not attempt to copy any of the images and/or text found on the computer.

Law Enforcement Prevention and Protection Efforts

A coordinated effort among law enforcement agencies globally is necessary to effectively combat this growing worldwide problem. For example, the United States, United Kingdom, Australia and Canada, have established the Virtual Global Taskforce (VGTB) to prevent and deter child abuse on the Internet. One of the deterrent actions taken by VGTB—known as Operation PIN—is the creation of a Web site that purports to contain images of child abuse.

Anyone who enters the site and attempts to download images is met with various warnings about the criminality of their actions. The individual is finally informed that they have entered a law enforcement Web site, has committed a crime, and the details of his or her offense are being forwarded to appropriate local law enforcement authorities.

In addition, special software is available to law enforcement agencies which identifies clues in images that may be helpful in tracing both the child and the abuser. Additional international prevention and enforcement efforts are being implemented globally.

Federal Legislation

In addition to the Children's Internet Protection Act (CIPA), there are three other federal statutes designed to protect children using the Internet.

Use of a Computer Service to Display Obscenity to Minors

It is illegal to knowingly use an interactive computer service to display obscenity or child pornography in a manner that makes it available to a person under 18:

> **Obscene or harassing telephone calls in the District of Columbia or in interstate or foreign communications (47 U.S.C. § 223)**
>
> **(d) Sending or displaying offensive material to persons under 18**
>
> Whoever—
>
> > (1) in interstate or foreign communications knowingly—
> >
> > > (A) uses an interactive computer service to send to a specific person or persons under 18 years of age, or
> > >
> > > (B) uses any interactive computer service to display in a manner available to a person under 18 years of age, any comment, request, suggestion, proposal, image, or other communication that is obscene or child pornography, regardless of whether the user of such service placed the call or initiated the communication; or
> >
> > (2) knowingly permits any telecommunications facility under such person's control to be used for an activity prohibited by paragraph (1) with the intent that it be used for such activity—
>
> shall be fined under title 18 or imprisoned not more than two years, or both.

Making Obscene Commercial Communications Available to Minors

In prohibiting obscene commercial communications to minors, Congress found that there was a compelling government interest in protecting the physical and psychological well-being of minors by shielding them from materials that are harmful to them.

Acknowledging that the custody and care of the child resides first with the parent, Congress reasoned that the widespread availability of the Internet presents opportunities for minors to access obscene materials in a manner that can frustrate parental supervision or control. Congress recognized that despite the innovative ways the industry has found to restrict the access of minors to adult Web sites, these efforts have not yet provided a national solution to the problem.

Thus Congress found that the most effective and least restrictive means by which they could satisfy this compelling government interest was by prohibiting the distribution of material harmful to minors, combined with the availability of legitimate defenses.

Pursuant to the statute, it is illegal to knowingly make a commercial communication via the Internet that includes obscenity and is available to any minor under age 17. However, the statute includes an affirmative defense for an individual or entity that has attempted, in good faith, to restrict access by minors using age verification procedures.

Restriction of access by minors to materials commercially distributed by means of World Wide Web that are harmful to minors 17 (47 U.S.C. § 231)

(a) Requirement to restrict access

(1) Prohibited conduct—Whoever knowingly and with knowledge of the character of the material, in interstate or foreign commerce by means of the World Wide Web, makes any communication for commercial purposes that is available to any minor and that includes any material that is harmful to minors shall be fined not more than $50,000, imprisoned not more than 6 months, or both.

(2) Intentional violations—In addition to the penalties under paragraph (1), whoever intentionally violates such paragraph shall be subject to a fine of not more than $50,000 for each violation. For purposes of this paragraph, each day of violation shall constitute a separate violation.

(3) Civil penalty—In addition to the penalties under paragraphs (1) and (2), whoever violates paragraph (1) shall be subject to a civil penalty of not more than $50,000 for each violation. For purposes of this paragraph, each day of violation shall constitute a separate violation.

(c) Affirmative defense—

(1) Defense—It is an affirmative defense to prosecution under this section that the defendant, in good faith, has restricted access by minors to material that is harmful to minors—

(A) by requiring use of a credit card, debit account, adult access code, or adult personal identification number;

(B) by accepting a digital certificate that verifies age; or

(C) by any other reasonable measures that are feasible under available technology.

(2) Protection for use of defenses—No cause of action may be brought in any court or administrative agency against any person on account of any activity that is not in violation of any law punishable by criminal or civil penalty, and that the person has taken in good faith to implement a defense authorized under this subsection or otherwise to restrict or prevent the transmission of, or access to, a communication specified in this section.

Using Internet Domain Names to Mislead Minors

It is illegal to use Internet domain names with the intent to mislead a minor into viewing material that is harmful to minors, or to mislead any person into viewing obscenity.

Misleading Domain Names on the Internet (18 U.S.C. § 2252B)

(a) Whoever knowingly uses a misleading domain name on the Internet with the intent to deceive a person into viewing material constituting obscenity shall be fined under this title or imprisoned not more than 2 years, or both.

(b) Whoever knowingly uses a misleading domain name on the Internet with the intent to deceive a minor into viewing material that is harmful to minors on the Internet shall be fined under this title or imprisoned not more than 10 years, or both.

(c) For the purposes of this section, a domain name that includes a word or words to indicate the sexual content of the site, such as "sex" or "porn," is not misleading.

(d) For the purposes of this section, the term "material that is harmful to minors" means any communication, consisting of nudity, sex, or excretion, that, taken as a whole and with reference to its context—

(1) predominantly appeals to a prurient interest of minors;

(2) is patently offensive to prevailing standards in the adult community as a whole with respect to what is suitable material for minors; and

(3) lacks serious literary, artistic, political, or scientific value for minors.

(e) For the purposes of subsection (d), the term "sex" means acts of masturbation, sexual intercourse, or physical contact with a person's genitals, or the condition of human male or female genitals when in a state of sexual stimulation or arousal.

PORNOGRAPHIC SPAM E-MAIL

Unsolicited commercial e-mail (UCE) is informally known as "spam." If the e-mails are pornographic, i.e., they typically link to pornographic Web sites, this is known as "porn spam." In 2003, Congress enacted a law that seeks to control non-solicited pornography.

In passing this law, Congress recognized that: (1) there is a substantial government interest in regulation of commercial electronic mail (spam); (2) senders of spam should not mislead recipients as to the source or content of such mail; and (3) recipients of spam have a right to decline to receive additional spam from the same source.

Congress further found that spam has become the method of choice for those who distribute pornography, as well as those who perpetrate fraudulent schemes, and introduce viruses into personal and business computer systems.

CAN-SPAM Act of 2003 (Public Law 108-187)

In 2003, Congress enacted the Controlling the Assault of Non-Solicited Pornography and Marketing Act of 2003, commonly referred to as the CAN-SPAM Act of 2003.

The CAN-SPAM Act contains a number of important provisions that are designed to deter and punish those who seek to send "porn spam."

The Act amends the Federal criminal code to impose a fine, imprisonment, or both, on any person who:

1. accesses a protected computer without authorization and intentionally initiates the transmission of multiple commercial electronic mail messages from or through such computer;

2. uses a protected computer to relay or retransmit multiple messages, with the intent to deceive or mislead recipients or any Internet access service as to the origin of such messages;

3. materially falsifies header information in multiple messages and intentionally initiates the transmission thereof;

4. registers, with materially false identifying information, for five or more electronic mail accounts or online user accounts or two or more domain names, and intentionally initiates the transmission of multiple messages from such accounts or domain names; or

5. falsely represents oneself to be the registrant or legitimate successor in interest to the registrant of five or more Internet protocol addresses and intentionally initiates the transmission of multiple messages from such addresses.

The Act also provides for higher penalties in the case of offenses committed in furtherance of any felony, or if the defendant has previously been convicted for conduct involving the transmission of multiple messages or unauthorized access to a computer system. The violator may also be required to forfeit any property obtained from such an offense, and the equipment, software, or other technology used to commit the offense.

The Act sets forth protections against spam that include the following:

1. a prohibition against false or misleading transmission information;

2. a prohibition against deceptive subject headings;

3. mandatory inclusion of a return address or a comparable mechanism in commercial electronic mail;

4. A prohibition against transmission of spam after objection, including a prohibition against transferring or releasing an e-mail address after an objection;

5. mandatory inclusion in spam of information identifying the message as an advertisement or solicitation, notice of the opportunity to decline to receive further unsolicited messages from the sender, and the sender's physical address;

6. a prohibition against initiating transmission of spam to a protected computer, or assisting in the origination of such message through the provision of addresses, if the person had actual knowledge, or knowledge fairly implied on the basis of objective circumstances, that the recipient's address was obtained from an Internet Web site or proprietary online service that included a notice that the operator will not provide addresses for initiating unsolicited messages;

7. a prohibition against using automated means to register for multiple e-mail accounts for the transmission of spam; and

8. a prohibition against relaying or retransmitting an unsolicited message that is unlawful under this section.

The Act also requires a person, when initiating commercial electronic mail containing sexually oriented material, to provide labels warning of the content, unless the recipient has given prior affirmative consent to receipt of such mail. Violators are subject to criminal penalties.

Selected provisions of the CAN-SPAM Act can be found in Appendix 4, "The CAN-SPAM Act of 2003 [Pub. L. No. 108-187, 12/16/2003], of this Almanac.

Taking Action Against Unsolicited Pornographic Spam

If you receive unsolicited pornographic spam, you should never reply to the sender. In addition, you should not follow any instructions that advise you how to remove your name from their "list." This only serves to alert the spammer that you have a valid e-mail address that they can sell to other spammers.

In addition, you should file a complaint with your local and state law enforcement authorities, asking them to start an investigation. You should also contact your Internet Service Provider (ISP) to report the incident, and to the sender's Internet Service Provider. Most ISPs have policies prohibiting spam and will shut down the account of anyone who violates the policy.

CHAPTER 3:
THE PORNOGRAPHY INDUSTRY

IN GENERAL

The business of the pornography industry generally includes the production and distribution of magazines, videocassettes, DVDs, and films; computer sex services; peep shows; and telephone services, commonly referred to as "dial-a-porn."

There is really no incentive to stop producing and distributing pornography. Everyone in the distribution chain is making money in this multi-billion dollar industry, including the telephone company, which has expanded its operations in order to handle the volume of "dial-a-porn" calls.

Due in large part to changing moral standards over the last fifty years, the audience has broadened. Pornographic materials are readily available. No longer does an individual have to travel to a dangerous, seedy part of town to find X-rated films, magazines, and other pornographic materials. Cable television, satellite television, video rentals, computers, and telephone services bring a vast array of X-rated materials to the consumer in the privacy of his or her home.

Opponents of pornography contend that a number of crimes are directly and indirectly related to the pornography industry, including murder, rape, physical violence, prostitution, sexual abuse, and drugs. Further, the profits reaped from the industry are often used to support other criminal activities.

Anti-pornography community activists have attempted to halt some of the operations, particularly those operating in public, such as adult bookstores and peep shows. By staging pickets of these establishments, they have had some success. However, the bottom line is that as long as there are consumers willing to support the pornography industry, it will thrive and prosper.

NATURE OF THE BUSINESS

Pornography is big business. The profit margin for the producers and distributors of pornography is enormous. In the United States, revenue from the pornography industry exceeded $13 billion dollars in 2006. Globally, pornography revenues exceeded $97 billion dollars in 2006. Some speculate that pornography is the most profitable business on the Internet.

The pornography industry is so lucrative, that some of the nation's largest and most conventional companies are getting in on the action. Most people are aware of adult video stores, pornographic magazines, peep shows, and Internet pornography. The lesser known companies that are profiting from pornography include legitimate businesses, such as major hotel chains and cable and satellite companies.

For example, nearly all of the major hotel chains, such as Hilton and Marriott, offer in-room X-rated movies. The hotel receives a portion of the revenue from the distribution companies that supply the programming without laying out any costs of their own. Thus it is a 100% profit venture for the hotel.

In addition, cable and satellite companies offer X-rated movies to consumers who subscribe to designated pay-per-view stations. It is estimated that the companies receive 80% of the revenue. Such well-respected companies as AT&T (AT&T Broadband) and General Motors (DirecTV) were involved in X-rated adult programming until they sold off those interests to other companies.

THE ROLE OF ORGANIZED CRIME

Law enforcement officials contend that significant parts of the pornography industry are controlled by organized crime due to its lucrative nature. In 1986, the Attorney General's Commission on Pornography (1986), commonly referred to as the "Meese Report," investigated the role of organized crime in the pornography industry.

According to testimony given by the Chief of the Los Angeles Police Department, organized crime infiltrated the pornography industry in Los Angeles in 1969 due to the financial benefits. An additional monetary incentive was the fact that a large part of the pornography business operated on a cash basis—e.g., no cash receipts for merchandise. Thus profits were easily hidden from the Internal Revenue Service, making the industry even more attractive to criminal enterprises.

By 1975, it was estimated that organized crime controlled 80% of the industry, and by 1986, the figure was estimated to be between 85 and 90%. Organized crime families from Chicago, New York, New Jersey, and Florida were openly controlling and directing the major pornography operations in Los Angeles, where the majority of obscene and pornographic materials are produced.

Organized crime expanded by forming film and video duplication companies that illegally duplicated the films of independent producers and displayed them at nationwide organized crime controlled theaters. They forced independent retailers out of business through price manipulation. Those dealers who protested were silenced by means of extortion and arson.

The term "organized crime" is generally defined as a large and organized enterprise engaged in criminal activity, with a continuity, a structure, and a defined membership, that is likely to use other crimes and methods of corruption, such as extortion, assault, murder, or bribery, in the service of its primary criminal enterprise. Although at one time the term was almost exclusively used to refer to the Mafia, today it includes many more criminal syndicates that operate in this country.

According to the FBI, these highly organized criminal organizations include "Eurasian Organized Crime," which consists of criminals born in or with family from the former Soviet Union or Central Europe (a/k/a the "Russian Mafia"), as well as a number of Asian criminal enterprises that operate in at least 50 major U.S. cities. These groups are also lured into the sex business by its profitable nature.

According to experts in the field, sexual exploitation today has grown into an extremely lucrative enterprise. It is estimated that the sex industry, including pornography, child pornography, prostitution, and sex trafficking, brings in anywhere from $7 billion to $57 billion a year. However, due to the nature of the business, it is difficult to provide exact figures.

These criminal enterprises play a dominant role in the pornography industry, and have expanded their business to include trafficking in sex slaves. Young women and children are lured from all areas of the world, particularly Asia and Eastern Europe, and brought to the United States where they are forced into pornography and prostitution.

The United Nations estimates that the number of women and children who are sexually exploited by the sex trade industry each year is approximately one million, while child-advocacy groups, estimate that there are currently two million children worldwide that are working as sex slaves.

THE MOVIE INDUSTRY

Most legitimate motion picture companies do not produce the kinds of films that would be considered "pornographic." As discussed in Chapter 6, "Protecting Your Children: Ratings Systems and the Media," of this Almanac, the legitimate motion picture industry has voluntarily established a rating system for mainstream movies, and producers and distributors are concerned with the rating that their productions are given by the Motion Picture Association of America (MPAA).

Producers and distributors of pornographic films do not share the same concern over ratings as do the producers and distributors of legitimate films. In fact, it is unlikely that they would even submit their films to the MPAA. Such films can hardly be considered as having any legitimate artistic value, as they contain little or no plot, graphic and explicit sexual activity, and have no purpose other than to provide sexual arousal.

Usually, the producers and distributors of pornographic movies will self-designate their films with a number of Xs—e.g., XXX—for no legitimate reason other than to attract those viewers who are interested in watching extremely graphic or explicit sexual activity.

Approximately 80% of the American production of adult movies and videos takes place in and around Los Angeles, California. In part, this is a consequence of the location there of technical personnel, such as camera operators, who either are, have been, or wish to be employed in the mainstream motion picture industry.

Indeed, this description applies as well to many of the performers in these films, although, unlike technical personnel, the likelihood of a performer who is involved in pornographic movies simultaneously or eventually working in the mainstream motion picture industry is minuscule.

Production of these movies tends to be done on a rather limited budget, usually in temporary locations such as motel rooms or rented houses, and usually in quite a short period of time. Often, not only the premises, but the photographic equipment as well, is rented for only the limited time necessary to make the film. It is not uncommon for producer, director, and scriptwriter to be the same person.

Distribution

Because of the low production costs—e.g., $5,000 to $10,000—the adult film business is quite lucrative. Small production companies can make huge profits in distribution. Video distribution is on a national scale, and most of that national distribution is controlled by a relatively limited number of companies. These distributors duplicate the movies in large quantities and then sell them to wholesalers, who in turn sell the videos to home video rental stores that carry adult entertainment. Videos are also licensed to pay-per-view cable and satellite stations.

Child Pornography

The illegal production of movies using children engaged in sexual activity is largely distinct from the industry of producing sexually explicit movies involving adults. The "producers" of child pornography are child molesters who abuse children for their own perverted desires. The trade in child pornography is among pedophiles via mail and the Internet. Production of such materials is not connected to any legitimate commercial industry.

Child pornography is discussed more fully in Chapter 4, "Child Pornography," of this Almanac.

THE TELEVISION INDUSTRY

Broadcast television is generally prohibited from televising frontal nudity and explicit sexual activity, although it certainly contains a fair amount of sexual themes and innuendo. As discussed in Chapter 5, "FCC Regulation of Broadcast Media," of this Almanac, the Federal Communications Commission (FCC) is responsible for enforcing the laws that ensure decency in broadcasting.

Thus far, the FCC has not enforced the indecency and profanity provisions against subscription programming services such as cable and satellite television, although it does enforce the prohibition against obscenity against such services.

Nevertheless, cable and satellite programming is replete with sexually explicit programming, including talk shows specializing in sexual themes; music videos featuring strong sexual and violent themes; cable channels that specialize in sexual material; and more general purpose cable channels that offer mainstream motion pictures that would not be shown on broadcast television in their uncut version.

Although some movies available on cable might be deemed legally obscene in some areas, and although much of this material is highly explicit and offensive, the sexually explicit material available on cable has not been determined to be legally obscene.

THE MAGAZINE INDUSTRY

Although the sexual content of large numbers of so-called mainstream magazines continues to increase, magazines deemed "pornographic" are often those that fall into the category of "men's magazines." These magazines vary enormously in sexual content and explicitness.

For example, a few magazines of this variety combine their sexual content with a substantial amount of non-sexually oriented, and frequently quite serious, textual or photographic matter. However, the majority of these magazines feature significant amounts of simulated or actual sexual activity, and graphic and sexually explicit images.

While the sexually explicit, and sometimes sexually violent, content of many of these magazines can hardly be considered "legally obscene," they generally circulate around the country with little, if any, legal attack.

Distribution

Adult-oriented magazines are usually produced and distributed in a similar manner to the production and distribution methods for most mass-circulation magazines. The magazines are distributed nationally, and are generally first sold to wholesalers who, in turn, sell the magazines to retailers. Many of the magazines are also sold by mail, usually as a result of advertisements placed in similar magazines.

"ADULTS ONLY" RETAIL ESTABLISHMENTS

Most pornographic material reaches the consumer through retail establishments specializing in adult material. These outlets, commonly referred to as "adults only" establishments, usually limit entry to those eighteen years of age or older, but the strictness of the enforcement of the limitation to adults varies considerably.

Some of these retail establishments specialize in videos and magazines. Increasingly, however, the "peep show," is often combined with an outlet for the sale of pornographic videos and magazines. The typical peep show is located on the premises of an "adults only" establishment selling large numbers of pornographic magazines and videos, along with other items, such as sexual paraphernalia. The peep show is often separated from the rest of the establishment, and consists of a number of booths in which an adult video can be viewed by the customer for a fee.

COMMUNITY INVOLVEMENT

Many concerned citizens are understandably upset when an "adults only" enterprise sets up shop in their community. There is widespread agreement that virtually all such establishments are largely detrimental to the neighborhoods in which they are located. They invite an unsavory clientele, and are often accompanied by illegal activities, such as prostitution.

These types of businesses are certain to bring down property values and negatively affect home sales in the community. Community activists are continually looking for legal ways to protect their community from the influx of undesirable businesses, and shield their children from exposure to such activities. Citizen involvement in law enforcement and the formulation of legal initiatives can help strengthen and protect the integrity of the community.

Zoning Regulations and Nuisance Laws

Although some communities have tried to deal with sexually-oriented enterprises through criminal prosecution, others have attempted to use zoning regulations. Zoning regulations generally take two forms.

One type of zoning ordinance is a "dispersal" regulation, in which the law prohibits the location of such an establishment within a specified distance of another establishment of the same type. The goal of a dispersal ordinance is to scatter these establishments throughout a large geographic area so that there is no major detrimental effect on any one neighborhood.

Alternatively, some communities have attempted to use zoning regulations to limit these establishments to one or two locations within the community, usually located in a remote area away from residential areas, and frequently distant from the mainstream business districts.

In order for these zoning ordinances to be effective, the statute must be able to describe the establishments they regulate in terms at least slightly broader than the *Miller* definition of obscenity. Most such ordinances, therefore, regulate establishments that specialize in sexually explicit material, and usually the ordinance contains a definition of sexually explicit material that is more precise but more expansive than *Miller* test, discussed in Chapter 1, "An Overview of Obscenity Law," of this Almanac.

The Supreme Court has approved zoning regulations of this variety. The most significant qualification imposed by the Court is the requirement that the zoning regulation not have the effect of a total prohibition. The result, therefore, is that if communities wish to restrict the location of such "adults only" establishments, they may do so, but they may not under the guise of zoning banish them altogether.

For this reason, trying to regulate these establishments through the use of "nuisance" laws is generally found unconstitutional when challenged. Nuisance laws as applied to businesses that offer sexually explicit material are seen as mere attempts to prohibit these establishments, unlike zoning ordinances that seek relocation. If the community does not yet have any sexually-oriented businesses operating as of yet, it is advisable to pass a zoning law in order to deter any businesses from locating there in the future.

Grandfather Exemptions

In many states, "grandfather exemptions" allow non-conforming businesses that existed prior to the effective date of the zoning ordinance to remain in business even though the law has changed. Thus in order to prevent such a businesses from locating in a particular community, the zoning ordinance should contain a clause that would restrict the transfer of existing, non-conforming businesses, if possible.

Restrictions on Public Display

Many localities try to regulate obscene or offensive materials by placing restrictions on the manner in which such sexually explicit materials may be displayed in public. In this way, unwilling viewers are not subjected to offensive images and children are protected from exposure to materials that are not age appropriate. The restriction extends to billboards and advertising, and generally requires a retail outlet to shield sexually explicit magazine covers.

Criminal Prosecution

Obscenity is illegal whether it is found in a sexually-oriented outlet or a mainstream video store. However, law enforcement agencies generally do not have the time or manpower to police all of these establishments. Therefore, in many communities, concerned citizens have formed watch groups to monitor such activities. In this endeavor, it is important to know your federal and state obscenity laws and what the law prohibits. The federal obscenity statutes are set forth at United States Code, Title 18, Chapter 71, Sections 1460–1470.

State laws exist in over 40 states that criminalize the sale or rental of obscene materials, including magazines, films, videos, and books.

In states where no obscenity laws exist, you must rely on the federal law, if applicable, and coordinate efforts to obtain state legislation.

A table setting forth state obscenity statutes can be found in Appendix 5, "State Obscenity Statutes," of this Almanac.

Members of community groups formed to prevent obscenity and pornography in their neighborhood may visit these businesses and, if it appears that there are materials available at the establishment that would be deemed statutorily obscene, a report should be made to the appropriate federal and state law enforcement agencies, requesting a criminal investigation.

This tactic has been encouraged by anti-pornography activist organizations, such as ObscenityCrimes.org, which has designed obscenity reporting forms for individuals and groups to use in reporting violations.

Sample state and federal obscenity reporting forms can be found in Appendix 6, "State Obscenity Report Form," and Appendix 7, "Federal Obscenity Report Form," respectively, of this Almanac.

Community Action Initiatives

The Meese Commission advised that citizens should consider the following methods to fight against the influx of sexually-oriented businesses in their community.

1. Citizens concerned about pornography in their community can establish and maintain effective community action organizations.

2. Community action organizations can support from a broad spectrum of civic leaders and organizations.

3. Community action organizations can gather information about pornography in their community.

4. Community action organizations can educate the public about the effect pornography has on their community.

5. Community action organizations can communicate with law enforcement officials and prosecutors about the pornography in their jurisdiction.

6. Citizens can file complaints, when appropriate, with the Federal Communications Commission about obscene broadcasts.

7. Community action organizations can conduct a "Court Watch" program. Citizens involved in a "Court Watch" program will often sit through a court hearing or trial. They will write to the prosecutor,

judge, or police officer and relay their opinions of the investigation, prosecution, and disposition of the case. "Court Watch" participants will also relay their findings to other interested parties, the media, and legislators. In addition, these individuals will often publicly disseminate the information they have gathered when officials come up for re-appointment or re-election.

8. Community action organizations are encouraged to remain informed of developments in obscenity and pornography-related laws and may wish, when appropriate, to lobby for legislative changes and initiatives.

9. Community action organizations can provide assistance and support to local, state and federal officials in the performance of their duties.

10. Citizens can use grassroots efforts to express opposition to pornographic materials to which they object.

11. Citizens can exercise their economic power by patronizing individual businesses and corporations that demonstrate responsible judgment in the types of materials they offer for sale.

12. Parents should monitor the music their children listen to and the recording artists and producers should use discretion in the fare they offer to children.

13. All institutions that are taxpayer-funded should prohibit the production, trafficking, distribution, or display of pornography on their premises or in association with their institution to the extent constitutionally permissible.

14. Businesses can actively exercise their responsibility as "corporate citizens" by supporting their community's effort to control pornography.

A successful community action program should contain the following components:

1. citizen interest in controlling the proliferation of pornographic material in their community;

2. a police department that is willing to allocate a reasonable portion of its resources to obscenity enforcement;

3. a prosecutor who will aggressively pursue violations of obscenity statutes with due regard for the right to distribute constitutionally protected material; and

4. a judiciary that is responsive to obscenity violations and will sentence offenders appropriately.

STOPPING UNWANTED SEXUALLY ORIENTED ADVERTISING BY U.S. MAIL

If you receive unwanted sexually oriented advertising in your mail, or are concerned about your minor children being exposed to such advertising, there are two programs you can use to help protect yourself and your children.

Prohibitory Order

Pursuant to the Pandering Advertisements Statute (39 U.S.C. § 3008), if you are the addressee of an advertisement, and consider the material— e.g., an invitation for a product or service—to be "erotically arousing or sexually provocative," you can obtain a Prohibitory Order that directs the mailer to make no mailings whatsoever to anyone named in the Order, effective on the 30th calendar day after the mailer receives it.

You can obtain a Prohibitory Order by submitting the entire original advertisement, along with the completed Application for a Listing and/ or Prohibitory Order, to the U.S. Postal Service. Minor children under 19 years old and residing with you may be included in the application. If the addressee is a minor, you may apply for an order in your minor child's name. If the addressee is a deceased person whose mail you are entitled to receive, you may apply for an order in the deceased's name.

Listing Order

Pursuant to the Sexually Oriented Advertisements Statute (39 U.S.C. § 3010), the U.S. Postal Service maintains a list of persons who do not wish to receive sexually oriented advertisements in the mail. Applicants for this list may also have their minor children less than 19 years of age, who are residing with them or are under their care, custody, or supervision, included on the list.

The statute defines the term "sexually oriented advertisement" essentially as an advertisement depicting or explicitly describing human genitalia, sexual intercourse, sadistic or masochistic acts, or related erotic subjects, and prohibits mailing such an advertisement to those whose names and addresses have been on the list for more than 30 days.

You can be placed on the list by submitting an Application for a Listing and/or Prohibitory Order to the U.S. Postal Service. Because being added to the list does not depend on having received a sexually oriented advertisement, you do not need to submit any pieces of mail with your completed application. If you wish to have a listing for more than one address, you must complete a separate application for each address.

Violations

When your application has been processed, the U.S. Postal Service will notify you of the effective date of your protected status and how to report any violation. Your obtaining the protection offered through these two programs makes sending prohibited mail to you unlawful. However, it does not make such mailings physically impossible.

If you receive a piece of mail that appears to violate your Order, contact your local post office or refer to your notification letter for instructions on submitting the piece of mail as evidence for possible enforcement action.

A sample U.S. Postal Service Application for a Listing and/or Prohibitory Order can be found in Appendix 8, "USPS Application for Listing and/or Prohibitory Order," of this Almanac.

CHAPTER 4:
CHILD PORNOGRAPHY

IN GENERAL

According to the U.S. Department of Justice, the trafficking of child pornography within the United States was practically eradicated by the mid 1980s. Law enforcement agencies were able to successfully crack down on child pornographers. It became too difficult and expensive to reproduce the illicit images, and distributing child pornography was extremely risky. This made it hard for pedophiles to engage in trading child pornography.

Unfortunately, with the tremendous advances in technology that followed, there was a resurgence in child pornography that could not have previously been imagined, much less anticipated. Now, pornographic images and movies of children have flooded the Internet, and are easily accessible to any perverted individual who has access to a computer.

The distribution of child pornography over the Internet is inexpensive and can be accomplished with virtual anonymity. It is relatively easy to upload these images and transmit them worldwide within minutes by even the most inexperienced computer user. The volume of child pornography available through the Internet presents an overwhelming task for law enforcement to combat.

THE U.S. DEPARTMENT OF JUSTICE

The Child Exploitation and Obscenity Section (CEOS) of the U.S. Department of Justice was created in 1987 to enforce the federal criminal statutes relating to the exploitation of children and obscenity. The CEOS, with its staff of experts in child exploitation and obscenity, assists the 93 U.S. Attorney Offices in investigating these offenses. They work together to successfully prosecute the individuals who violate the federal laws related to producing, distributing, receiving, or possessing child pornography; transporting women or children interstate for the purpose of engaging in criminal sexual activity; traveling interstate or internationally to sexually abuse children; and transporting obscene materials in interstate or foreign commerce.

In addition, the CEOS takes aggressive action to protect children from those individuals who use computers and the U.S. mail to sexually abuse and exploit them. In that endeavor, the CEOS works closely with the Federal Bureau of Investigation (FBI), the United States Bureau of Immigration and Customs Enforcement, the United States Postal Inspection Service, and the United States Secret Service.

Most recently, the CEOS, together with the FBI, initiated a major campaign to end the use of computers to traffic in child pornography and exploit children online. Insofar as the distribution of child pornography through the Internet is international in scope, the CEOS works closely with law enforcement officials of other countries to combat this growing problem. The CEOS also provides training on child pornography issues to the FBI and other law enforcement personnel.

CHILD PORNOGRAPHY DEFINED

The law defines child pornography as *the visual depiction of a person under the age of 18 engaged in sexually explicit conduct* (18 U.S.C. §§ 2256(1) and (8)). This means that any image of a child engaged in sexually explicit conduct is illegal contraband.

It should be noted that the legal definition of *sexually explicit conduct* does not require that an image depict a child engaged in sexual activity (18 U.S.C. § 2256(2)). For example, a picture of a naked child may constitute illegal child pornography if it is sufficiently sexually suggestive.

In addition, for purposes of the child pornography statutes, federal law considers *a person under the age of 18* to be a child (18 U.S.C. § 2256(1)). It is thus irrelevant that the age of consent for sexual activity in a given state might be lower than age 18. A majority of states follow the federal statute, however, some state laws define *minor* or *child* as a youth *younger than 14, 16, or 17*. Delaware law includes any person *18 years of age and younger* in its definition of a child.

A *visual depiction* for purposes of the federal child pornography statutes includes a photograph or videotape, including undeveloped film, as well as data stored electronically which can be converted into a visual image. For example, images of children engaged in sexually explicit conduct stored on a computer disk are considered visual depictions.

CHILD PORNOGRAPHY AND THE FIRST AMENDMENT

Case law has consistently held that the possession or distribution of child pornography is not protected under the First Amendment. The compelling interest of the state to protect children is paramount to the rights guaranteed under the First Amendment. Thus the U.S. Supreme Court routinely upholds laws protecting minors from sexual exploitation and child pornography.

New York v. Ferber

In *New York v. Ferber*, 458 U.S. 747 (1982), the U.S. Supreme Court upheld the constitutionality of a New York statute that prohibited persons from "knowingly promoting a sexual performance by a child under the age of 16 by distributing material which depicts such a performance." The Court stated:

> The New York statute describes a category of material the production and distribution of which is not entitled to First Amendment protection. Accordingly, there is nothing unconstitutionally "under-inclusive" about the statute, and the State is not barred by the First Amendment from prohibiting the distribution of such unprotected materials produced outside the State.

The Court also upheld restrictions on various depictions of minors that could be considered sexual, citing the compelling need to protect actual children from possible exploitation by child pornographers. The question remained unanswered, however, whether any such material that has literary, historical, scientific or artistic value would be protected. For example, the First Amendment does protect certain material that, under other circumstances, may be deemed pornographic, such as images of naked children in a medical book.

Osborne v. Ohio

In *Osborne v. Ohio*, 495 U.S. 103 (1990), the U.S. Supreme Court went even further in its endeavor to protect children, and upheld a law that criminalizes an adult's possession of child pornography in his own home.

Child Pornography Protection Act of 1996

In 1996, Congress attempted to strengthen the laws prohibiting the production and distribution of child pornography by including additional legislation in the Federal budget bill. The law was known as the

Child Pornography Protection Act of 1996 (CPPA), which was struck down as unconstitutional.

Prior to passage of the CPPA, illegal child pornography only involved depictions of actual children engaged in sexually explicit activity. The CPPA criminalized not only sexual images involving actual children, but also criminalized the use of computer-generated images; the use of adult "body doubles;" and sexual images that appeared to be minors or that were advertised as minors, even if no minors were actually involved. Violators of the law faced mandatory prison sentences of 15 years.

Thus the CPPA expanded the definition of illegal child pornography to include images not necessarily based on real children. The theory behind the law was that such images encourage pedophilia.

Opponents of the CPPA argued that the statute went too far because it did not recognize materials that may have artistic, historical, scientific, literary, or other value, as protected under the First Amendment. In addition, they argued that the law as written would criminalize movie scenes in which an adult was used to portray a minor engaged in sexual activity.

Ashcroft v. Free Speech Coalition

In *Ashcroft v. Free Speech Coalition*, 535 U.S. 234 (2002), the U.S. Supreme Court struck down the CPPA. The opponents' arguments focused on the difficulty of applying the law, pointing out that mainstream movies such as "Traffic," "Lolita," and "Titanic," would be illegal under the law, since they all had scenes depicting minors in sexual situations.

In a 6-to-3 ruling, the Supreme Court sided with the opponents of the statute, holding that the CPPA's scope was unconstitutionally overbroad. Justice Kennedy noted:

> The mere tendency of speech to encourage unlawful acts is not a sufficient reason for banning it . . . The Government has shown no more than a remote connection between speech that might encourage thoughts or actions and any resulting child abuse. Without a significantly stronger, more direct connection, the Government may not prohibit speech on the ground that it might encourage pedophiles to engage in illegal conduct.

Pandering and Solicitation Statute (18 U.S.C. § 2252A)

After the Supreme Court struck down the CPPA as facially overbroad, Congress passed a pandering and solicitation provision (18 U.S.C. § 2252A) that, as recently as May 2008, has withstood an attack on grounds that it is overbroad, vague, and violates the First Amendment.

The statute provides, in part:

Certain activities relating to material constituting or containing child pornography

(a) Any person who—

(1) knowingly mails, or transports or ships using any means or facility of interstate or foreign commerce or in or affecting interstate or foreign commerce by any means, including by computer, any child pornography;

(2) knowingly receives or distributes—

(A) any child pornography that has been mailed, or using any means or facility of interstate or foreign commerce shipped or transported in or affecting interstate or foreign commerce by any means, including by computer; or

(B) any material that contains child pornography that has been mailed, or using any means or facility of interstate or foreign commerce shipped or transported in or affecting interstate or foreign commerce by any means, including by computer;

(3) knowingly—

(A) reproduces any child pornography for distribution through the mails, or using any means or facility of interstate or foreign commerce or in or affecting interstate or foreign commerce by any means, including by computer; or

(B) advertises, promotes, presents, distributes, or solicits through the mails, or using any means or facility of interstate or foreign commerce or in or affecting interstate or foreign commerce by any means, including by computer, any material or purported material in a manner that reflects the belief, or that is intended to cause another to believe, that the material or purported material is, or contains—

(i) an obscene visual depiction of a minor engaging in sexually explicit conduct; or

(ii) a visual depiction of an actual minor engaging in sexually explicit conduct;

(4) either—

(A) in the special maritime and territorial jurisdiction of the United States, or on any land or building owned by, leased to, or otherwise used by or under the control of the United States Government, or in the Indian country (as defined in section 1151), knowingly sells or possesses with the intent to sell any child pornography; or

(B) knowingly sells or possesses with the intent to sell any child pornography that has been mailed, or shipped or transported using any means or facility of interstate or foreign commerce or in or affecting interstate or foreign commerce by any means, including by computer, or that was produced using materials that have been mailed, or shipped or transported in or affecting interstate or foreign commerce by any means, including by computer;

(5) either—

(A) in the special maritime and territorial jurisdiction of the United States, or on any land or building owned by, leased to, or otherwise used by or under the control of the United States Government, or in the Indian country (as defined in section 1151), knowingly possesses, or knowingly accesses with intent to view, any book, magazine, periodical, film, videotape, computer disk, or any other material that contains an image of child pornography; or

(B) knowingly possesses, or knowingly accesses with intent to view, any book, magazine, periodical, film, videotape, computer disk, or any other material that contains an image of child pornography that has been mailed, or shipped or transported using any means or facility of interstate or foreign commerce or in or affecting interstate or foreign commerce by any means, including by computer, or that was produced using materials that have been mailed, or shipped or transported in or affecting interstate or foreign commerce by any means, including by computer;

(6) knowingly distributes, offers, sends, or provides to a minor any visual depiction, including any photograph, film, video, picture, or computer generated image or picture, whether made or produced by electronic, mechanical, or other means, where such visual depiction is, or appears to be, of a minor engaging in sexually explicit conduct—

(A) that has been mailed, shipped, or transported using any means or facility of interstate or foreign commerce or in or affecting interstate or foreign commerce by any means, including by computer;

(B) that was produced using materials that have been mailed, shipped, or transported in or affecting interstate or foreign commerce by any means, including by computer; or

(C) which distribution, offer, sending, or provision is accomplished using the mails or any means or facility of interstate or foreign commerce, for purposes of inducing or persuading a minor to participate in any activity that is illegal; or

(7) knowingly produces with intent to distribute, or distributes, by any means, including a computer, in or affecting interstate or foreign commerce, child pornography that is an adapted or modified depiction of an identifiable minor shall be punished as provided in subsection (b).

(b)(1) Whoever violates, or attempts or conspires to violate, paragraph (1), (2), (3), (4), or (6) of subsection (a) shall be fined under this title and imprisoned not less than 5 years and not more than 20 years, but, if such person has a prior conviction under this chapter, section 1591, chapter 71, chapter 109A, or chapter 117, or under section 920 of title 10 (article 120 of the Uniform Code of Military Justice), or under the laws of any State relating to aggravated sexual abuse, sexual abuse, or abusive sexual conduct involving a minor or ward, or the production, possession, receipt, mailing, sale, distribution, shipment, or transportation of child pornography, or sex trafficking of children, such person shall be fined under this title and imprisoned for not less than 15 years nor more than 40 years.

(2) Whoever violates, or attempts or conspires to violate, subsection (a)(5) shall be fined under this title or imprisoned not more than 10 years, or both, but, if such person has a prior conviction under this chapter, chapter 71, chapter 109A, or chapter 117, or under section 920 of title 10 (article 120 of the Uniform Code of Military Justice), or under the laws of any State relating to aggravated sexual abuse, sexual abuse, or abusive sexual conduct involving a minor or ward, or the production, possession, receipt, mailing, sale, distribution, shipment, or transportation of child pornography, such person shall be fined under this title and imprisoned for not less than 10 years nor more than 20 years.

(3) Whoever violates, or attempts or conspires to violate, subsection (a) (7) shall be fined under this title or imprisoned not more than 15 years, or both.

(c) It shall be an affirmative defense to a charge of violating paragraph (1), (2), (3)(A), (4), or (5) of subsection (a) that—

(1)(A) the alleged child pornography was produced using an actual person or persons engaging in sexually explicit conduct; and

(B) each such person was an adult at the time the material was produced; or

(2) the alleged child pornography was not produced using any actual minor or minors.

U.S. v. Williams

In a recent case, *U.S. v. Williams*, 128 S. Ct. 1830, 170 L.Ed.2d 650 (2008), the respondent plead guilty to the pandering and solicitation statute, but reserved the right to challenge his pandering conviction's constitutionality.

The District Court rejected his challenge, but the Eleventh Circuit reversed, finding the statute both overbroad under the First Amendment and impermissibly vague under the Due Process Clause.

On appeal, the U.S. Supreme Court upheld the constitutionality of the provision, holding that the statute was not overbroad under the First Amendment:

A statute is facially invalid if it prohibits a substantial amount of protected speech. Section 2252A . . . generally prohibits offers to provide and requests to obtain child pornography. It targets not the underlying material, but the collateral speech introducing such material into the child-pornography distribution network. Its definition of material or purported material that may not be pandered or solicited precisely tracks the material held constitutionally proscribable in *New York* v. *Ferber* . . . and *Miller* v. *California* . . . : obscene material depicting (actual or virtual) children engaged in sexually explicit conduct, and any other material depicting actual children engaged in sexually explicit conduct . . . Offers to engage in illegal transactions are categorically excluded from First Amendment protection.

The Court also held that the statute was not impermissibly vague under the Due Process Clause:

> The Eleventh Circuit mistakenly believed that "in a manner that reflects the belief" and "in a manner . . . that is intended to cause another to believe" were vague and standardless phrases that left the public with no objective measure of conformance. What renders a statute vague, however, is not the possibility that it will sometimes be difficult to determine whether the incriminating fact it establishes has been proved; but rather the indeterminacy of what that fact is . . . There is no such indeterminacy here. The statute's requirements are clear questions of fact. It may be difficult in some cases to determine whether the requirements have been met, but courts and juries every day pass upon the reasonable import of a defendant's statements and upon "knowledge, belief and intent."

The ACLU Position on Child Pornography and the First Amendment

The American Civil Liberties Union (ACLU) is a strong proponent of First Amendment rights. Ironically, despite the ACLU's condemnation of child exploitation, their advocacy of the First Amendment has placed them on the side of the child pornography industry on a number of occasions.

The ACLU has taken the position that control of the child pornography industry should not be fought on First Amendment grounds, but that the preferred method should be by implementing stricter statutory controls governing child sexual abuse.

The ACLU argues that, by using this tactic, the actual offenders—i.e., the producers of child pornography—would be prosecuted for engaging in illegal behavior. The ACLU believes that the publishers and distributors of the material should not be held accountable as they are protected under the First Amendment.

Of course, the ACLU has many critics who denounce their reasoning, maintaining that the First Amendment does not protect all printed material, and, in no event, should it ever protect child pornographers.

FEDERAL JURIDICTION OVER INTERSTATE AND FOREIGN COMMERCE

Distribution of Child Pornography Across State Lines

Federal prosecutors enforce the laws that make it a crime to possess, receive, distribute, or produce child pornography in a way that affects interstate or foreign commerce (18 U.S.C. §§ 2251, 2252, 2252A).

Thus federal jurisdiction is implicated when the visual image is transported across state lines, or when the visual image was produced using materials that were transported across state lines.

This prohibition includes transporting pornographic materials depicting children electronically by computer. For example, it is illegal under federal law to send an e-mail containing child pornography to a person in another state. It is also illegal to send an e-mail containing child pornography to a person in the same state if the computer server for the e-mail is located in a different state.

Distribution of Child Pornography on the Internet

It is a violation of federal law to download child pornography from an Internet Web site. Even in cases where the image itself has not traveled in interstate or foreign commerce, federal law may still be violated if the materials used to create the image—e.g., the DVD on which the child pornography is stored—travels in interstate or foreign commerce.

Distribution of Child Pornography through the U.S. Postal Service

It is a violation of federal law to use the U.S. Postal Service to mail child pornography, even if the material is mailed to someone in the same state. In addition, use of the U.S. mail to lure a child into engaging in prostitution or criminal sexual activity also constitutes a federal offense.

Transmitting a Child's Personal Information

Further, it is a federal crime for any person to use the mail or any facility or means of interstate or foreign commerce to knowingly transmit the name, address, telephone number, social security number, or e-mail address of a child under the age of 16 with the intent to lure the child to take part in prostitution or other criminal sexual activity (18 U.S.C. § 2425).

Selling or Purchasing Children for Sexual Activity

It is a violation of federal law to sell or purchase children with the intent or knowledge that the child will be involved in any sexual activity (18 U.S.C. § 2251A). Federal prosecutors have legal authority to prosecute people who buy and sell children for pornographic or sexual activity when the child being sold or transferred must be transported in interstate or foreign commerce, or when the offer to sell or purchase the child is communicated or transported in interstate or foreign commerce by any means, including computer or U.S. mail.

Child Trafficking for Participation in Sexual Activity

It is a violation of federal law for any person to knowingly transport a child in interstate or foreign commerce intending that the child become a prostitute or take part in any sexual activity constituting a criminal offense (18 U.S.C. §§ 1591, 2421–2423). This prohibition includes importing an alien for such purposes.

For example, it is a crime for an adult, who finds a child in a chat room, to use e-mails to persuade the child to meet in person, with the intent that the child engage in sexual activity. Even if the child does not have to cross a state line to meet the pedophile, the pedophile could be prosecuted under federal law if the computer server used in the e-mail was located in a different state

Engaging in Sexual Activity With a Child

It is a violation of federal law for any person to travel between states or abroad for the purpose of engaging in any sexual act with a child (18 U.S.C. § 2423). For example, it is a federal crime for an adult U.S. citizen to travel abroad to a foreign country to engage in sexual activity with a citizen of that foreign country under the age of 18. It is also a crime to *attempt* to engage in this type of activity.

Liability of Internet Service Providers

The Protection of Children from Sexual Predators Act of 1998 (the "Sexual Predators Act") requires an Internet Service Provider (ISP) to notify a designated law enforcement agency after learning that a Web site containing child pornography exists on its server. If the ISP willfully fails to report the Web site, the ISP can be fined.

STATE LAW

In their "parens patrie" role as guardians of abused and/or neglected children, the state has the primary interest in protecting its children. Virtually all states have laws that prohibit the production and distribution of child pornography. Thus individuals who possess, receive, distribute, or produce child pornography may be prosecuted under state laws in addition to, or instead of, federal law. In addition, in those cases where interstate conduct does not occur, state and local law enforcement authorities can prosecute the responsible parties.

A table of state child pornography statutes can be found in Appendix 9, "State Child Pornography Statutes," of this Almanac.

New York State Penal Law

The New York Penal Law is an example of a comprehensive set of state statutes prohibiting the production, promotion, and possession of child pornography.

Offenses

§ 263.05 Penal. Use of a child in a sexual performance

A person is guilty of the use of a child in a sexual performance if, knowing the character and content thereof he employs, authorizes or induces a child less than seventeen years of age to engage in a sexual performance or being a parent, legal guardian or custodian of such child, he consents to the participation by such child in a sexual performance

Use of a child in a sexual performance is a class C felony.

§ 263.10 Penal. Promoting an obscene sexual performance by a child.

A person is guilty of promoting an obscene sexual performance by a child when, knowing the character and content thereof, he produces, directs or promotes any obscene performance which includes sexual conduct by a child less than seventeen years of age.

Promoting an obscene sexual performance by a child is a class D felony.

§ 263.11 Penal. Possessing an obscene sexual performance by a child.

A person is guilty of possessing an obscene sexual performance by a child when, knowing the character and content thereof, he knowingly has in his possession or control any obscene performance which includes sexual conduct by a child less than sixteen years of age.

Possessing an obscene sexual performance by a child is a class E felony.

§ 263.15 Penal. Promoting a sexual performance by a child.

A person is guilty of promoting a sexual performance by a child when, knowing the character and content thereof, he produces, directs or promotes any performance which includes sexual conduct by a child less than seventeen years of age.

Promoting a sexual performance by a child is a class D felony.

§ 263.16 Penal. Possessing a sexual performance by a child.

A person is guilty of possessing a sexual performance by a child when, knowing the character and content thereof, he knowingly has in his possession or control any performance which includes sexual conduct by a child less than sixteen years of age.

Possessing a sexual performance by a child is a class D felony.

Affirmative Defenses

The New York Penal Law provides for certain affirmative defenses to the above-described offenses. For example, it is an affirmative defense if the defendant, in good faith, reasonably believes that the child was over the prohibited age:

§ 263.20 Penal. Sexual performance by a child; affirmative defenses.

1. Under this article, it shall be an affirmative defense that the defendant in good faith reasonably believed the person appearing in the performance was, for purposes of section 263.11 or 263.16 of this article, sixteen years of age or over or, for purposes of section 263.05, 263.10 or 263.15 of this article, seventeen years of age or over.

The New York Penal Law also provide an affirmative defense for individuals employed in certain positions who are not responsible for producing, promoting or distributing the banned materials, and did not receive any compensation related to these activities:

§ 263.20 Penal. Sexual performance by a child; affirmative defenses.

2. In any prosecution for any offense pursuant to this article, it is an affirmative defense that the person so charged was a librarian engaged in the normal course of his employment, a motion picture projectionist, state employee or spotlight operator, cashier, doorman, usher, candy stand attendant, porter or in any other non-managerial or non-supervisory capacity in a motion picture theatre; provided he has no financial interest, other than his employment, which employment does not encompass compensation based upon any proportion of gross receipts, in the promotion of a sexual performance for sale, rental or exhibition or in the promotion, presentation or direction of any sexual performance, or is in any way responsible for acquiring such material for sale, rental or exhibition.

Proof of Age

In addition, in cases where it is difficult to determine whether the child who is the subject of exploitation is under the legal age, the New York Penal law provides a method whereby the trier of fact is able to make this determination:

§ 263.25 Penal. Proof of age of child.

Whenever it becomes necessary for purposes of this article to determine whether a child who participated in a sexual performance was under an age specified in this article, the court or jury may make such determination by any of the following: personal inspection of the child; inspection of a photograph or motion picture which constituted the sexual performance; oral testimony by a witness to the sexual performance as to the age of the child based upon the child's appearance; expert medical testimony based upon the appearance of the child in the sexual performance; and any other method authorized by any applicable provision of law or by the rules of evidence at common law.

Administration of a Controlled Substance or Alcohol

The New York Penal Law also prohibits the administration of a controlled substance or alcohol to a child to facilitate the sexual performance by the child:

§ 263.30 Penal. Facilitating a sexual performance by a child with a controlled substance or alcohol.

1. A person is guilty of facilitating a sexual performance by a child with a controlled substance or alcohol when he or she:

(a)(i) knowingly and unlawfully possesses a controlled substance as defined in section thirty-three hundred six of the public health law or any controlled substance that requires a prescription to obtain, (ii) administers that substance to a person under the age of seventeen without such person's consent, (iii) intends to commit against such person conduct constituting a felony as defined in section 263.05, 263.10, or 263.15 of this article, and (iv) does so commit or attempt to commit such conduct against such person; or

(b)(i) administers alcohol to a person under the age of seventeen without such person's consent, (ii) intends to commit against such person conduct constituting a felony as defined in section 263.05, 263.10, or 263.15 of this article, and (iii) does so commit or attempt to commit such conduct against such person.

2. For the purposes of this section, "controlled substance" means any substance or preparation, compound, mixture, salt, or isomer of any substance defined in section thirty-three hundred six of the public health law.

Facilitating a sexual performance by a child with a controlled substance or alcohol is a class B felony.

THE NATIONAL CENTER FOR MISSING AND EXPLOITED CHILDREN (NCMEC)

In 1996, the U.S. Congress established the Exploited Child Division within the National Center for Missing & Exploited Children (NCMEC). The Exploited Child Division serves as a resource center for the public, parents, and law enforcement, concerning the sexual exploitation of children. In this capacity, the Exploited Child Division carries out a number of important services, as set forth below.

1. The NCMEC processes reports received through the Cyber-Tipline regarding the sexual exploitation of children and provides leads to federal, state, local, and international law-enforcement agencies for further investigation.

2. The NCMEC provides technical assistance to federal, state, local, and international law-enforcement agencies that investigate child sexual exploitation cases.

3. The NCMEC maintains a database of law enforcement officers who have developed an expertise in investigating cases of child sexual exploitation.

4. The NCMEC works collaboratively with specialized units within the Federal Bureau of Investigation (FBI); the U.S. Immigration and Customs Enforcement; the U.S. Postal Inspection Service; the U.S. Secret Service; and the Bureau of Alcohol, Tobacco and Firearms, regarding the leads received through the Cyber-Tipline.

The Cyber-Tipline

The Cyber-Tipline is a mechanism that was mandated by Congress for the purpose of reporting cases of child sexual exploitation including child pornography, online enticement of children for sex acts, molestation of children outside the family, sex tourism of children, child victims of prostitution, and unsolicited obscene material sent to a child. The Cyber-Tipline is maintained by the NCMEC and funded by the U.S. Department of Justice.

Incidents involving the possession, distribution, receipt, or production of child pornography should be reported to the Cyber-Tipline (http://www.missingkids.com/) or by telephone (1-800-843-5678). Reports may be made 24-hours a day/7 days a week. The report will be forwarded to a law enforcement agency for investigation and action.

A table of Cyber-Tipline Annual Report Totals (1/1/06 through 12/31/06) can be found in Appendix 10, "Cyber-Tipline Annual Report Totals [1/1/06-12/31/06]," of this Almanac.

Reporting Child Pornography on the Internet

The FBI has primary jurisdiction for investigating child pornography on the Internet. They operate a very aggressive and highly successful national initiative known as "Innocent Images," that targets online child pornographers.

The FBI solicits the assistance of the public in reporting child pornography encountered on the Internet. According to the FBI, if you encounter any evidence of child pornography while online, you should do the following:

1. Note the name of the Web site, chat room, or newsgroup where you saw the suspected child pornography.

2. If you receive child pornography through unsolicited e-mail, note the sender's screen name and Internet Service Provider (ISP) and forward the entire message in your complaint. Do not copy and paste the message in the e-mail.

3. Do not download the child pornography to your computer.

4. File a report with the Cyber-Tipline as indicated above.

In December 1999, new legislation was passed title (42 U.S.C. 13032 (b)(1)) that requires Internet Service Providers (ISPs) to report child pornography and child sexual exploitation directly to the Cyber-Tipline.

THE FBI 2257 AGE VERIFICATION PROGRAM

Congress recognized the need to ensure that performers in sexually explicit material are of legal age in order to protect the sexual exploitation of minors. Thus legislation was enacted (18 U.S.C § 2257) to require producers of sexually explicit material to maintain certain records verifying the identity and age of performers. This requirement helps to ensure that producers will not exploit minors, either through carelessness, recklessness, or deliberate indifference.

In enforcing this law, the FBI is responsible for conducting random inspections at the places of business of producers of sexually explicit material without advance notice. This is known as the "2257 Program."

When the FBI inspector arrives at the producer's place of business, he or she is required to identify himself or herself, display FBI credentials, and explain the purpose and scope of the inspection. Photographs are taken of the exterior of the business, the location of the 2257 records storage, and the location where the records are examined.

Certain 2257 records are reviewed and copied, and the FBI inspector completes an inspection checklist regarding the producer's 2257 compliance. Inspectors compare clips from the reviewed material with the photo identification on file, and record the performers' true names and dates of birth.

If any violations are found, the FBI inspector prepares an informal preliminary report, and discusses the violations with the producer. The producer is given the opportunity to resolve the violations prior to the submission of the final inspection report that is submitted to the U.S. Department of Justice.

THE PROTECT ACT OF 2003

The PROTECT Act of 2003 was enacted in order to strengthen law enforcement's ability to prevent, investigate, prosecute, and punish violent crimes committed against children. The acronym "PROTECT" stands for Prosecutorial Remedies and Other Tools to end the Exploitation of Children Today.

The PROTECT Act established the AMBER Alert Program, which has proven to be an effective tool in helping to recover abducted children. The Act also abolished the statute of limitations for prosecuting offenders who abduct or abuse children. In addition, the law makes it more difficult for defendants accused of serious crimes against children to obtain bail.

Under the Act, the penalties for the sexual exploitation of children and child pornography were increased. A first offense of using a child to produce child pornography is now 15 to 30 years. In addition, a "two strikes" provision requires life imprisonment for offenders who commit two serious sexual abuse offenses against a child.

The Act also limits a judge's ability to give a defendant a reduced prison sentence, by eliminating the grounds of "downward departure," such as "diminished capacity," "aberrant behavior," and "family and community ties."

For example, in one child pornography case, a judge departed downward from the mandatory sentence, in part, on the ground that the defendant had a "diminished capacity" due to the fact that he "was extremely addicted to child pornography." The Act ensures that pedophiles will not be able to get reduced sentences just because they are pedophiles.

The Act also extends the term of supervised release of sex offenders from five years to any term of years, even for life. This is due to the high rate of recidivism for sex offenders.

In addition, the Act revises and strengthens the prohibition on "virtual" child pornography—i.e., material whose production may not have involved the use of real children; prohibits any obscene materials that depict children; and provides tougher penalties compared to existing obscenity law. The Act also encourages greater voluntary reporting of suspected child pornography found by Internet Service Providers on their systems.

FEDERAL PENALTIES

As discussed above, Congress has recently strengthened the penalties for violation of the federal laws related to child pornography. Mandatory and minimum sentences have been extended, as set forth below.

1. Production of Child Pornography (18 U.S.C. § 2251): Mandatory Minimum—15 years/Maximum—30 Years

2. Selling or Buying Children for Sexual Exploitation (18 U.S.C. § 2251A): Mandatory Minimum—30 years/Maximum—Life Imprisonment

3. Possession, Distribution and Receipt of Child Pornography (18 U.S.C. § 2252): Mandatory Minimum for Distribution or Receipt—5 years/Maximum—20 Years

4. Possession, Distribution and Receipt of Child Pornography (18 U.S.C. § 2252A): Mandatory Minimum for Distribution or Receipt—5 years/Maximum—20 Years

5. Importation of Child Pornography (18 U.S.C. § 2260): Maximum—10 Years

THE NATURE OF THE CHILD PORNOGRAPHY INDUSTRY

The structure of the child pornography industry ranges from individual abusers who are out to satisfy their own perverted desires to highly organized, profit-seeking operations, many of which are suspected to have a connection with organized crime.

Profile of the Child Pornographer

According to the Attorney General's Commission on Pornography, child pornographers come from a broad range of religious, educational, ethnic, and socioeconomic backgrounds and occupations. Offenders often exhibit low self-esteem and difficulty relating intimately with others.

The Commission has defined child pornographers as either "situational" or "preferential" molesters:

A *situational molester* is one who acts out of some serious sexual or psychological need, but who chooses children as victims only when they are readily and safely accessible.

The *preferential molester*, also known as a *pedophile,* exhibits a clear sexual preference for children, and the offender's deviant desires can only be satisfied by children.

These behaviors have been noted by experts to be an addiction which, like other addictive behaviors, can be controlled but not cured.

Statistics—2000/2001

According to the NCMES, almost all of the approximately 1,713 child pornography possessors arrested between July 1, 2000 and June 30, 2001 were male; 91% were white; and 86% were older than 25. Only 3% were younger than 18. Most were unmarried at the time of their crime, either because they had never married (41%) or because they were separated, divorced, or widowed (21%). Thirty-eight (38%) percent were either married or living with partners.

Most of those individuals who were arrested possessed graphic images explicitly showing sexual acts by or on children. Ninety-two (92%) percent had images of minors focusing on genitals or showing explicit sexual activity; 80% had pictures showing the sexual penetration of a child, including oral sex; 71% possessed images showing sexual contact between an adult and a minor, defined as an adult touching the genitals or breasts of a minor or vice-versa; 21% had child pornography depicting violence such as bondage, rape, or torture and most of those involved images of children who were gagged, bound, blindfolded, or otherwise enduring sadistic sex; and 79% also had what might be termed "softcore" images of nude or semi-nude minors.

In addition, more than 1 in 3 (39%) of those individuals arrested had child-pornography videos with motion and sound. Approximately one-half (48%) of those individuals arrested had more than 100 graphic still images, and 14% had 1,000 or more graphic images.

Further, 40% of those individuals arrested were dual offenders who sexually victimized children and possessed child pornography, with both crimes discovered in the same investigation. An additional 15% were dual offenders who attempted to sexually victimize children by soliciting undercover investigators who posed online as minors.

Profile of the Child Victim

Child victims also come from a wide variety of family backgrounds, including all socioeconomic classes and religions. They range in age from infancy through adolescence.

Young children are often victimized by someone they know, e.g., a neighbor or family member. Many crave adult affection, and are lured into the behavior in an effort to obtain approval by adult authority figures. Others are kidnapped by strangers and forced into submission.

Adolescent victims are often runaways or teens engaged in criminal behavior, such as prostitution. Their economic situation is usually precarious, and many are homeless. The pornographers prey on their vulnerability, often luring them with money and a place to stay.

Statistics—2000/2001

According to the NCMES, most of the children depicted in the images possessed by the individuals arrested between July 1, 2000 and June 30, 2001 were pre-pubescent. Eighty-three (83%) percent of those arrested had images of children between the ages of 6 and 12; 39% had images of children aged 3 to 5; and 19% had images of toddlers or infants younger than age 3.

The Process of Producing Child Pornography

Following are common steps reportedly taken by child pornography producers in introducing a child to pornographic activity:

1. Pornographic materials are shown to the child victim, e.g., for sex education purposes.

2. An attempt is made to convince the child victim that sex is acceptable and desirable.

3. Showing of child pornography is used to convince the child victim that other children are sexually active.

4. The showing of child pornography to the child victim desensitizes the child and lowers the child's inhibitions.

5. Sexual activity may occur during sessions.

6. Photographs or movies are taken of the sexual activity.

Effects of Child Pornography on the Victims

The immediate effects of child pornography on the victims include physical injuries, such as genital bruising, lacerations, and exposure to sexually transmitted diseases. However, the long-term effects on these children are devastating. These children also suffer from depression, anger, and psychological disorders. They are generally unable to form normal sexual relationships with persons of the opposite sex.

In addition, many child victims fall into destructive lifestyles, such as drug and alcohol addiction, and many succumb to suicide. They are also subject to continual re-victimization because these graphic images are often traded on the Internet among pedophiles, and can remain in circulation on the World Wide Web indefinitely.

CHILD PROSTITUTION

Child prostitution is generally defined as the sexual exploitation of a child for remuneration in case or in-kind, usually but not always organized by an intermediary, such as a procurer, family member, pimp, or madam.

Child prostitution is another form of child sexual abuse closely related to child pornography. In fact, children who are forced into or voluntarily engage in prostitution are also often used in producing pornography.

Child prostitution involves both male and female children. Victims of child prostitution have been reported to be as young as age 9, and at least 25% of prostitutes are under the age of 18.

Children who are subjected to sexual exploitation generally suffer from long-term psychological problems, such as depression with suicidal tendencies, disassociation, and post-traumatic shock. They often turn to drugs or alcohol to escape the trauma.

CHAPTER 5:
FCC REGULATION OF BROADCAST MEDIA

THE FEDERAL COMMUNICATIONS COMMISSION (FCC)

The Federal Communications Commission (FCC) is responsible for enforcing the laws that ensure decency in broadcasting. The FCC is careful to carry out this mission without infringing on the First Amendment protections contained in the U.S. Constitution, and the prohibitions on censorship and freedom of speech in broadcasting set forth in Section 326 of the Communications Act.

Thus far, the FCC has not enforced the indecency and profanity provisions against subscription programming services such as cable and satellite television, although it does enforce the prohibition against obscenity against such services.

Most of the FCC staff responsible for processing, reviewing, and investigating allegations of obscenity, indecency and/or profanity are located in the Consumer and Government Affairs Bureau (CGB) and the Enforcement Bureau (EB). The EB employs attorneys and support personal that work on the hundreds of thousands of complaints they receive each year alleging violations of the restrictions on obscene, indecent, or profane programming.

THE CENSORSHIP MOVEMENT

Most censorship movements target violent and sexual content in the media as unprotected forms of expression under the First Amendment. Proponents of censorship argue that violent images on television may cause people, and children in particular, to act in more aggressive and destructive ways.

If it could be proven that exposure to violence in the media resulted in violent actions in real life, there would be a compelling reason to censor such images. However, opponents argue that there is no evidence that fictional violence causes otherwise balanced people to become violent.

Scientific studies on the correlation between violence in the media and actual violence have been conducted and are subject to debate. Children who have been exposed to violent television programming have been shown to temporarily act more aggressively during play following this exposure. However, the problem with any study is the old "chicken and the egg" quandary—it is nearly impossible to determine whether individuals who are already prone to aggression are also drawn to violent programming, or whether the violent programming causes the aggressive behavior.

Proponents of censorship have attempted to limit sexual content in the television industry. Although the Supreme Court has allowed censorship of "sexual speech" on moral grounds, not all sexual expression can be suppressed, and only a narrow range of obscene materials are restricted. Although the Supreme Court has held that indecent expression is entitled to some degree of constitutional protection, it has held that indecency in some media may be regulated.

Federal Communications Commission v. Pacifica Foundation

In *Federal Communications Commission v. Pacifica*, 438 U.S. 726 (1978), the Court ruled that the government could require radio and television stations to broadcast "indecent" material only during programming hours when children would be least likely to view or listen. The Court defined "broadcast indecency" as "language that describes, in terms patently offensive as measured by contemporary community standards for the broadcast medium, sexual or excretory activities or organs."

VIOLATIONS

The United States Code (18 U.S.C. § 1464) prohibits the utterance of any obscene, indecent or profane language by means of radio communication. It is a violation to air obscene programming at any time, and a violation to broadcast indecent or profane programming during certain hours of the day (6:00 a.m. to 10:00 p.m.).

Obscenity Violation

As discussed in Chapter 1, "An Overview of Obscenity Law," of this Almanac, to be considered obscene, material must meet a three-prong test formulated by the U.S. Supreme Court:

1. an average person, applying contemporary community standards, must find that the material, as a whole, appeals to the prurient interest;

2. the material must depict or describe, in a patently offensive way, sexual conduct specifically defined by applicable law; and

3. the material, taken as a whole, must lack serious literary, artistic, political, or scientific value.

Obscene materials are not protected by the First Amendment. Therefore, broadcasters may not air obscene programming at any time whatsoever.

Indecency Violation

Material is considered indecent if, in contest, it depicts or describes sexual or excretory organs or activities in terms that are patently offensive as measured by contemporary community standards for the broadcast medium. Thus in determining whether certain material is indecent, the FCC must satisfy two prongs:

1. whether the material describes or depicts sexual or excretory organs or activities; and

2. if so, whether the material is patently offensive.

The second prong of the indecency test is the more difficult to determine. Thus in order to determine whether certain material is patently offensive, the FCC looks at three primary factors:

1. whether the description or depiction is explicit or graphic;

2. whether the material dwells on or repeats at length descriptions or depictions of sexual or excretory organs; and

3. whether the material appears to pander or is used to titillate or shock.

The FCC must weigh and balance these three factors in making its determination. No single factor is determinative of whether a particular broadcast is indecent.

Because the material is not deemed obscene, indecent material is not entirely prohibited because it is protected by the First Amendment. However, restrictions may be imposed in order to protect children from exposure to indecent material.

For example, it is permissible to restrict the airing of indecent material to certain times of the day when it is less likely that children will be listening or viewing the material. The FCC has determined that there is a reasonable risk of exposure to children during the hours of 6:00 a.m. and 10:00 p.m. Thus licensees are prohibited from broadcasting indecent material during these hours, referred to as the "safe harbor."

Profanity Violation

Language that is deemed profane includes words that are so highly offensive that their mere utterance in the context presented, in legal terms, amounts to a "nuisance." Like indecent material, profane language may not be broadcast during 6:00 a.m. and 10:00 p.m. in order to prevent exposing children to such language.

The FCC determines whether a profanity violation has taken place on a case-by-case basis, depending on the context in which the particular word or words were spoken.

FILING A COMPLAINT

The FCC does not monitor radio and television programming in order to determine whether violations have taken place. The FCC enforces the prohibitions on obscenity, indecency, and profanity based on the complaints it receives from the public about a particular program or performer.

In making its determination as to whether certain material is obscene, indecent, or profane, the FCC analyzes: (1) what was actually aired; (2) the meaning of what was aired; and (3) the context in which it was aired. Thus the FCC asks complainants to provide information regarding the details of what was actually said or depicted during the program.

Sufficient Details

A complainant must provide the FCC with sufficient detail as to the words or language used, or the images or scenes depicted, and the context in which the words, language, images, or scenes were used. Merely complaining about the subject matter will not suffice, e.g., the program was "about explicit sex."

The complainant is not required to provide a tape or transcript to support the allegations in the complaint. However, a tape or transcript is helpful in investigating the complaint, and should be provided, if available. Nevertheless, the failure to provide a tape or transcript will not lead to an automatic dismissal or denial of the complaint.

Date and Time of Broadcast

The complainant must include the date and time of the program in the complaint. As set forth above, indecent or profane speech that is broadcast between 6:00 a.m. and 10 p.m. is prohibited. In addition, the law requires the FCC to specify the date a violation occurred in order to assess a monetary penalty against a broadcast station. Thus date and time are important factors the FCC must consider when making its determination and enforcing the law.

Broadcast Channel, Call Sign or Frequency

The complainant must include the call sign, channel, or frequency of the station involved in the complaint. The FCC must be able to identify the station that aired the material in order to take enforcement action. Additional specifics are also helpful including the name of the program, on-air personality, song, or film; the network; the city and state where the program was heard, etc.

Where to File a Complaint

A complaint may be filed as follows:

1. online at the FCC Web site (esupport.fcc.gov/complaints.htm);

2. e-mail (fccinfo@fcc.gov);

3. telephone (voice): 1-888-CALL-FCC (1-888-225-5322);

4. telephone (TTY): 1-888-TELL-FCC (1-888-835-5322);

5. fax: 1–866–418–0232

A complaint may also be filed by writing to the FCC at the following address:

> Federal Communications Commission
> Consumer & Governmental Affairs Bureau
> Consumer Inquiries and Complaints Division
> 445 12th St., SW
> Washington, DC 20554

A sample FCC Complaint Form (FCC Form 475B) can be found in Appendix 11, "FCC Complaint Form," of this Almanac.

If you are submitting a videotape, DVD, CD, or other type of media with your complaint, you should send it to the following address to avoid mail processing damage:

> Federal Communications Commission
> Consumer & Governmental Affairs Bureau
> Consumer Inquiries and Complaints Division
> 9300 East Hampton Drive
> Capitol Heights, MD 20743

There is no fee for filing a complaint with the FCC.

The Complaint Process

When the FCC receives a complaint, the FCC staff scan or otherwise record it in a database. The complaint is then forwarded to the staff responsible for initial review. FCC staff reviews each complaint to determine whether it contains sufficient information to suggest that there has been a violation of the obscenity, indecency, or profanity laws.

If the complaint does not contain sufficient information to determine whether a violation has taken place, the FCC staff will send the complainant a dismissal letter explaining the deficiencies in the complaint and how to have it reinstated. In such a case, the complainant has the option of re-filing the complaint with additional information, filing a petition for reconsideration or, if the decision is a staff action, an appeal to the full Commission.

If the facts and information contained in the complaint suggest that a violation of the statute or FCC rules regarding obscenity, indecency, and profanity did not occur, the FCC staff will send the complainant a letter denying the complaint. Alternatively, the FCC may deny the complaint by public order. In either situation, the complainant has the option of filing a petition for reconsideration or, if the decision is a staff action, an appeal to the full Commission.

If it appears that a violation may have occurred, the FCC staff will start an investigation, which may include sending a Letter Of Inquiry (LOI) to the broadcast station. Depending on the case, an LOI may ask the station to confirm or deny the allegations in the complaint and provide copies of any tapes or transcripts of the program at issue.

Keeping Informed

A complainant can make sure he or she is kept informed of the status of the complaint by sending a copy of the complaint to the station that broadcast the offensive material, and informing the FCC that they have done so. By taking this action, the complainant becomes a party to the investigation. As a party, the complainant is entitled to copies of all written communications between the FCC and the station licensee, including any FCC letters of inquiry and licensee responses.

A complainant can also check on the status of the complaint by calling the FCC at (202) 418-1420. The complainant will be notified of the outcome of the FCC's investigation of the complaint in writing letter or by public order imposing a monetary sanction.

ENFORCEMENT

The FCC is authorized to assess civil monetary penalties, and to revoke or deny renewal of a broadcast license. In addition, instead of one single monetary penalty for a violation, the FCC may impose a monetary penalty for each indecent utterance during a single broadcast.

If the FCC determines the material is arguably obscene, the matter will be referred to the Department of Justice. The Department of Justice has authority to bring criminal prosecutions for the broadcast of obscene, indecent, or profane material. If convicted in a federal district court, violators may be subject to criminal fines and/or imprisonment.

Penalties

Presently, the base monetary sanction for violation of the indecency, profanity and/or obscenity provisions is $7,000 per violation. The statutory maximum per violation is $32,500. The fine may be adjusted upward based on such factors as the nature, circumstances, extent and gravity of the violation. The FCC also takes into consideration the violator's degree of culpability, history of prior offenses, and ability to pay.

Notice of Apparent Liability for Forfeiture

Any entity or person who has willfully or repeatedly violated the indecency, obscenity and/or profanity prohibitions is potentially liable for a forfeiture penalty—a monetary sanction paid to the United States Treasury. In order to impose this penalty, the FCC must issue a Notice of Apparent Liability for Forfeiture to the violator. The Notice must contain the FCC's preliminary findings and the amount of the proposed forfeiture. The findings are based on a preponderance of the evidence that the entity or person violated the prohibitions.

The entity or person who is subject to the forfeiture penalty has the right to respond, in writing, and provide an explanation as to why the penalty should not be imposed. However, if the FCC nevertheless determines that there has been a violation, a formal forfeiture order imposing the monetary sanction will be issued.

CHAPTER 6:
PROTECTING YOUR CHILDREN: RATINGS SYSTEMS AND THE MEDIA

IN GENERAL

Children these days are exposed to violent and sexual images, as well as profane language, at younger and younger ages. They are able to download music and movies from the Internet, and have access to television programming 24 hours a day, 7 days a week. They may be exposed to video and computer games that glorify violent crime and display explicit sexual content.

It is virtually impossible for parents to preview every movie or television program that their child watches; to listen to every song their child hears; or to play every video game their child purchases. In an effort to provide parents with greater oversight and control, these industries have established methods to educate parents as to the content of various forms of media to which children may be exposed. Technology has also enabled parents to effectively block broadcast and cable television programs that are deemed inappropriate for children.

In addition, the motion picture, television and video game industries have established ratings systems that alert parents to the content and age appropriateness of the movies, programs, and video games their children access. The music industry has also provided parents with some control over the music their child listens to by instituting a labeling system that warns parents of sexually explicit, profane, or violent lyrical content.

THE MOTION PICTURE INDUSTRY

In 1968, motion picture theater owners established the motion picture rating system. The motion picture industry was the first in the entertainment business to voluntarily enforce its guidelines. It is estimated that most theater owners in the United States observe the rating system.

The full-time Motion Picture Rating Board consists of 10 to 13 members who serve for various lengths of time. There are no special qualifications for Board membership, except that the members must have a shared parenthood experience, must be possessed of an intelligent maturity, and most of all, have the capacity to put themselves in the role of most American parents so they can view a film and apply a rating that most parents would find suitable and helpful in aiding their decisions about their children and what movies they see.

The Rating Board works for the Classification and Rating Administration. The Chairman of the Motion Picture Association of America (MPAA) chooses the Chairman of the Rating Board to eliminate pressure upon the Board by outside influences.

The Rating Board is funded by fees charged to producers and distributors for the rating of their films. They are not forced to submit a film to the Board for rating, but the vast majority of producers and distributors decide to do so. If a producer or distributor decides not to have their film rated, they can release the film without a rating, or with any symbol or description they choose, as long as the symbol or description cannot be confused with the MPAA ratings.

In order to assign a rating for a particular movie, the Board views the film and discusses it as a group. Each member then completes a rating form giving his or her reason for the rating. There are many factors considered when assigning a rating to a movie including sex, violence, nudity, language, adult topics, and drug use. The rating is then decided by majority vote.

If a film is assigned an unfavorable rating, the producer or distributor may edit and resubmit the film for another rating. The producer or distributor may also appeal the rating to the Rating Appeals Board, which is the final arbiter of ratings. The Rating Appeals Board comprises 14 to 18 members from the industry organizations that govern the rating system.

The Rating Appeals Board gathers to view the film and hear the appeal. After the screening, the producer or distributor whose film is being appealed explains why he or she believes the rating was wrongly decided.

The chairman of the Rating Board states the reason for the film and rating.

Following the presentation, the Rating Appeals Board discusses the appeal and then takes a secret ballot. It requires a two-thirds vote of those present to overturn a Rating Board decision. The decision of the Appeals Board is final and cannot be appealed.

Motion Picture Ratings

There are currently five ratings for motion pictures:

1. **G (General Audiences)**—A G-rated motion picture contains nothing in theme, language, nudity, sex, violence, or other matters that, in the view of the Rating Board, would offend parents whose younger children view the motion picture. The G rating is not a "certificate of approval," nor does it signify a "children's" motion picture.

Some snippets of language may go beyond polite conversation but they are common everyday expressions. No stronger words are present in G-rated motion pictures. Depictions of violence are minimal. No nudity, sex scenes, or drug use are present in the motion picture. All ages are admitted to a G-rated motion picture.

2. **PG (Parental Guidance Suggested)**—A PG-rated motion picture should be investigated by parents before they let their younger children attend. The PG rating indicates, in the view of the Rating Board, that parents may consider some material unsuitable for their children, and parents should make that decision.

The more mature themes in some PG-rated motion pictures may call for parental guidance. There may be some profanity and some depictions of violence or brief nudity. But these elements are not deemed so intense as to require that parents be strongly cautioned beyond the suggestion of parental guidance. There is no drug use content in a PG-rated motion picture.

3. **PG-13 (Parents Strongly Cautioned)**—A PG-13 rating is a sterner warning by the Rating Board to parents to determine whether their children under age 13 should view the motion picture, as some material might not be suited for them. A PG-13 motion picture may go beyond the PG rating in theme, violence, nudity, sensuality, language, adult activities or other elements, but does not reach the restricted R category.

The theme of the motion picture by itself will not result in a rating greater than PG-13, although depictions of activities related to a mature theme may result in a restricted rating for the motion picture. Any drug use will initially require at least a PG-13 rating. More than brief nudity will require at least a PG-13 rating, but such nudity in a PG-13 rated motion picture generally will not be sexually oriented. There may be depictions of violence in a PG-13 movie, but generally not both realistic and extreme or persistent violence.

A motion picture's single use of one of the harsher sexually derived words, though only as an expletive, initially requires at least a PG-13 rating. More than one such expletive requires an R rating, as must even one of those words used in a sexual context. The Rating Board nevertheless may rate such a motion picture PG-13 if, based on a special vote by a two-thirds majority, the Rating Board feels that most American parents would believe that a PG-13 rating is appropriate because of the context or manner in which the words are used or because the use of those words in the motion picture is inconspicuous.

4. **R (Restricted)**—An R-rated motion picture, in the view of the Rating Board, contains some adult material. An R-rated motion picture may include adult themes, adult activity, hard language, intense or persistent violence, sexually-oriented nudity, drug abuse or other elements, so that parents are counseled to take this rating very seriously.

Children under 17 are not allowed to attend R-rated motion pictures unaccompanied by a parent or adult guardian. Parents are strongly urged to find out more about R-rated motion pictures in determining their suitability for their children. Generally, it is not appropriate for parents to bring their young children with them to R-rated motion pictures.

5. **NC-17**—An NC-17 rated motion picture is one that, in the view of the Rating Board, most parents would consider patently too adult for their children 17 and under. No children will be admitted. NC-17 does not mean "obscene" or "pornographic" in the common or legal meaning of those words, and should not be construed as a negative judgment in any sense. The rating simply signals that the content is appropriate only for an adult audience.

An NC-17 rating can be based on violence, sex, aberrational behavior, drug abuse or any other element that most parents would consider too strong and therefore off-limits for viewing by their children.

Video Retailers

In the mid-1980s, as home videos grew in popularity, video retailers joined theater owners in implementing the voluntary guidelines of the rating system. Parents who relied on the rating system found that the information provided by the rating classifications were equally helpful in monitoring home videos. Ratings are displayed on both the entire home entertainment package as well as on the videocassettes and DVDs.

The Video Software Dealers Association (VSDA), the major trade association for video retailers in the United States, has adopted a policy that strongly endorses the observance of the voluntary movie rating system by video retailers.

Advertising

The motion picture industry tries to ensure that all advertising for rated films is appropriate for viewing by the general public. Therefore, all advertising for films must be submitted to the MPAA Advertising Administration prior to being released to the public.

Advertising materials include, but are not limited to, all print ads, radio and TV spots, press kits, outdoor advertising such as billboards, Internet sites, video or DVD packaging, and trailers for both theatrical and home video releases. Advertising that is targeted for an audience attending a "G" or "PG" feature will not be approved if it includes scenes depicting violence, sensuality, offensive language, or other material that most parents would find unacceptable for their younger children to see or hear.

Film companies do have the option, however, of creating advertising for a limited audience for whom the material is appropriate, i.e., "restricted" trailers, which may be shown only before "R" and "NC-17" films, restricted-access Internet sites, and television spots reserved for late-night audiences.

THE TELEVISION INDUSTRY

In 1996, the television industry created the TV Parental Guidelines, a voluntary rating system designed to give parents information about the content of television programs. All television shows are rated by the broadcast or cable industry, except for news, sports, and unedited movies on premium cable channels.

The TV rating system provides parents with information about the content and age-appropriateness of television programs. These ratings can be used in conjunction with the V-Chip blocking device contained in many television sets, and with the parental controls in cable set-top boxes, to filter out unwanted programs.

The television industry also created the TV Parental Guidelines Monitoring Board, which handles questions and comments on the rating system. The TV Parental Guidelines Monitoring Board is responsible for ensuring there is as much uniformity and consistency in applying the Parental Guidelines as possible and is comprised of experts from the television industry and public interest advocates. The Board also reviews complaints about specific program ratings to help ensure accuracy.

Television Ratings

There are currently seven ratings for television programs:

1. **TV-Y (All Children)**—This rating is for a program designed to be appropriate for all children. Whether animated or live action, the themes and elements in the program are specifically designed for a very young audience, including children from ages 2–6. This program is not expected to frighten younger children.

2. **TV-7 (Older Children)**—This rating is for a program designed for children age 7 and above. It may be more appropriate for children who have acquired the developmental skills needed to distinguish between make-believe and reality. Themes and elements in this program may include mild fantasy or comedic violence, or may frighten children under the age of 7. Therefore, parents may wish to consider the suitability of this program for their very young children.

3. **TV-Y7-FV (Older Children-Fantasy Violence)**—This rating is designed for a program where fantasy violence may be more intense or more combative than other programs in the TV-Y7 category.

4. **TV-G (General Audience)**—This rating is designed for a program that is appropriate for all ages. Although this rating does not signify a program designed specifically for children, most parents may let younger children watch this program unattended. It contains little or no violence, no strong language and little or no sexual dialogue or situations.

5. **TV-PG (Parental Guidance Suggested)**—This rating is for a program that contains material parents may find unsuitable for younger children. Many parents may want to watch it with their younger children. The theme itself may call for parental guidance and/or the program contains one or more of the following: moderate violence (V), some sexual situations (S), infrequent coarse language (L), or some suggestive dialogue (D).

6. **TV-14 (Parents Strongly Cautioned)**—This rating is for a program that contains some material parents would find unsuitable for children under 14 years of age. Parents are strongly urged to exercise greater care in monitoring this program and are cautioned against letting children under the age of 14 watch unattended. This program contains one or more of the following: intense violence (V), intense sexual situations (S), strong coarse language (L), or intensely suggestive dialogue (D).

7. **TV-MA (Mature Audience Only)**—This rating is for a program that is specifically designed to be viewed by adults and therefore may be unsuitable for children under 17. This program contains one or more of the following: graphic violence (V), explicit sexual activity (S), or crude indecent language (L).

Channel Blocking

V-Chip Technology

The FCC requires that all televisions measuring 13 inches or larger include the V-Chip technology that allows parents to block undesirable programs in order to protect children from exposure to obscene, indecent, or profane programming. This is known as "channel blocking," and applies to all new television sets manufactured on or after January 1, 2000.

The television rating appears in the corner of the television screen during the first 15 seconds of a program. Ratings are also included in television programming guides and the television listings in newspapers.

The rating is encoded into the programs, and the V-chip technology reads the encoded information and blocks the programs based on the channel blocking choices made by the parent.

Cable Subscribers

Lockboxes and Set-Top Boxes

Cable subscribers may request a lockbox from their cable company. The lockbox prevents viewing any channel on which objectionable programming may appear.

Some cable analog and advanced analog set-top boxes give customers the ability to block channels. In order to block a certain channel, the viewer enters a Personal Identification Number (PIN) using the set-top's remote control or keypad.

Digital set-top boxes provided by cable operators have parental control capabilities that allow customers to block programming based on certain criteria, such as time and date, channel, program title, TV rating and/or motion picture rating.

Scrambling and Blocking

Section 640 of The Communications Act requires a cable operator to scramble or fully block the audio and video portions of programming services that are not specifically subscribed to by a customer.

THE MUSIC INDUSTRY

Parents' groups and religious fundamentalists have attempted to challenge the content of popular music since the 1980s. In 1984, the Parents' Music Resource Center (PMRC) was formed to alert the public of "the growing trend in music towards lyrics that are sexually explicit, excessively violent, or glorify the use of drugs and alcohol." Senate hearings on obscenity and indecency in music were subsequently held, and the recording industry agreed to address the situation.

In 1985, the Recording Industry Association of America (RIAA), the PMRC, and the National Parent Teacher Association (National PTA) reached an agreement that certain music releases containing explicit lyrics, and explicit depictions of violence and sex, would be labeled so parents could make intelligent listening choices for their children.

Opponents of the labeling system argued that such restrictions were arbitrary and vague, and made it impossible for artists, record companies, and stores to understand whether or how the laws applied to them. They feared that a labeling system could lead to self-censorship to avoid any possibility of criminal prosecution. The correct remedy, they argued, was that those who object to certain music lyrics use their own free-speech rights—e.g., pickets and boycotts—to bring their view to the public that such lyrics are harmful.

The RIAA PAL Program

The RIAA has since provided record companies and artists with the labeling tools that alert parents to explicit content in music. In 1990, the RIAA set standards that made the PAL Logo uniform and conspicuous so that parents could more easily identify those recordings that may not be suitable for children.

The "Parental Advisory" is a notice to consumers that recordings identified by this logo may contain strong language or depictions of violence, sex or substance abuse ("Pal Content"). The PAL Program gives parents the ability to monitor the children's musical choices, while still upholding the constitutional right to freedom of expression that allows for unpopular speech and opposes censorship.

Under the PAL Program, individual record companies and artists decide which of their releases should receive a "PAL Notice" indicating that the release contains explicit content. Depending on a number of factors, a PAL Notice may take the form of the specific PAL Logo, or an additional indicator approved by the RIAA for such use.

For example, the artist and the record company may agree that there is musical and artistic credibility in the whole of a musical work even when the lyrics may be too explicit for mainstream distribution. In those instances, the PAL Logo is typically applied prominently to the outside of the permanent packaging. The Logo or a similar PAL Notice may also appear in advertising for the sound recording.

In 2006, the RIAA continued to update the PAL Program to take into account the explosion of digital music services and the ability of consumers to receive sound recordings delivered directly to their personal computer or mobile device. Nevertheless, recordings that receive a PAL Notice account for a fraction of the music being produced. For example, for the first six months of 2006, less than 5% of albums released by the major record companies carried the Logo.

The Labeling Determination

In most cases, the decision that a particular sound recording should receive a PAL Notice is made by each record company in conjunction with the artist. According to the RIAA, in making the determination as to whether a particular recording should bear a PAL logo or warning, the record labels and artist must consider the following:

1. that contemporary cultural morals and standards should be used in determining whether parents or guardians would find the sound recording suitable for children;

2. the context in which the material is used, as some words, phrases, sounds, or descriptions might be offensive to parents if spotlighted or emphasized, but might not offend if merely part of the background or a minimal part of the lyrics;

3. the context of the artist performing the material, as well as the expectations of the artist's audience;

4. that lyrics are often susceptible to varying interpretations, and that words can have different meanings and should not be viewed in isolation from the music that accompanies them;

5. that such a determination requires sensitivity and common sense, and that context, frequency, and emphasis are obviously important; isolated or unintelligible references to certain material might be insufficient to warrant labeling a particular sound recording as containing PAL Content;

6. that the standards apply in the case of a single track commercially released as well as to full albums; and

7. that a sound recording may contain strong language or depictions of violence, sex, or substance abuse, yet due to other factors involved, may not merit a designation as containing PAL Content.

Edited Versions

The RIAA recommends that, when practicable, the record label or artist create an edited version of a PAL Content sound recording that does not include all of the same content contained in the original, and that no longer merits a PAL Notice. However, not all potentially objectionable content must be removed from the edited sound recording. For example, some such content might be retained in order not to compromise artistic expression.

Music Videos and Concert Recordings

Record labels and artists are also expected to follow the standards as they pertain to audio-visual products that incorporate the sound recording, such as music videos and concert performances. Basically, any audio-visual product that contains a PAL Content sound recording shall also be deemed to contain PAL Content. However, the use of a sound recording that does not contain PAL Content shall not preclude a determination that the audio-visual product contains PAL Content. In making the determination, the sound recording and visual production should be reviewed as a whole.

Advertising

There are also guidelines and requirements when advertising music that contains PAL Content. The guidelines and requirements are designed to provide clear and conspicuous notice that recordings contain PAL Content and parental discretion is advised, as well as notice of whether there is an edited version of the particular recording.

Record Retailers

The RIAA does not represent the record retailers, but works closely with the National Association of Recording Merchandisers (NARM), the

Digital Media Association (DiMA), the wireless industry, and leading technology companies on this issue. Some retailers have in-store policies prohibiting the sale of records displaying the PAL Logo to music buyers younger than age 18. In addition, many online retailers are now implementing parental control mechanisms.

THE VIDEO GAME INDUSTRY

Certain groups, such as The Entertainment Consumers Association (ECA), oppose the restriction of video games based on content, and believe that bills attempting to curtail video game sales, rentals, or use based on content are generally constitutionally invalid and violate the Constitutional right of free speech and freedom of expression.

The Entertainment Software Rating Board (ESRB)

The Entertainment Software Rating Board (ESRB) is a non-profit, self-regulatory body established in 1994. The ESRB assigns computer and video game content ratings, enforces industry-adopted advertising guidelines and helps ensure responsible online privacy practices for the interactive entertainment software industry.

Presently, video game publishers are self-regulated through the ESRB. The rating system is voluntary, although virtually all games that are sold at retail in the United States and Canada are rated by the ESRB. Many retailers, including most major chains, have policies to only stock or sell games that carry an ESRB rating, and most console manufacturers will only permit games that have been rated by ESRB to be published for their platforms.

Video game publishers that voluntarily adhere to the ESRB rating system are legally bound to follow the Principles and Guidelines for Responsible Advertising Practices. There are also a number of requirements concerning packaging and advertising. If a video game publisher fails to properly label or advertise their product, the ESRB has the power to compel compliance and issue sanctions, including fines.

The ESRB Ratings

The ESRB ratings were developed through a collaborative effort involving child development and academic experts and parents. The ratings are designed to reflect the overall content of the game and age appropriateness of a particular game. The ESRB rating system consists of two parts: (1); the ESRB Rating Symbol; and (2) the ESRB Content Descriptors that indicate elements in the game that triggered the particular rating.

The ESRB Rating Symbol

The ESRB rating symbol appears on the front of the computer or video game. There are currently six ESRB rating categories.

1. **EC (Early Childhood)**—Titles rated "EC" have content that may be suitable for ages 3 and older. Contains no material that parents would find inappropriate.

2. **E (Everyone)**—Titles rated "E" have content that may be suitable for ages 6 and older. Titles in this category may contain minimal cartoon, fantasy or mild violence and/or infrequent use of mild language.

3. **E10+ (Everyone 10 and older)**—Titles rated "E10+" have content that may be suitable for ages 10 and older. Titles in this category may contain more cartoon, fantasy, or mild violence, mild language and/or minimal suggestive themes.

4. **T (Teen)**—Titles rated "T" have content that may be suitable for ages 13 and older. Titles in this category may contain violence, suggestive themes, crude humor, minimal blood, simulated gambling, and/or infrequent use of strong language.

5. **M (Mature)**—Titles rated "M" have content that may be suitable for persons ages 17 and older. Titles in this category may contain intense violence, blood and gore, sexual content and/or strong language.

6. **AO (Adults Only)**—Titles rated "AO" have content that should only be played by persons 18 years and older. Titles in this category may include prolonged scenes of intense violence and/or graphic sexual content and nudity.

The ESRB Content Descriptors

The ESRB Content Descriptors indicate the elements in the game that triggered the particular rating. There are approximately 30 different content descriptors that refer to potentially inappropriate content:

1. Alcohol Reference—Reference to and/or images of alcoholic beverages.

2. Animated Blood—Discolored and/or unrealistic depictions of blood.

3. Blood—Depictions of blood.

4. Blood and Gore—Depictions of blood or the mutilation of body parts.

5. Cartoon Violence—Violent actions involving cartoon-like situations and characters. May include violence where a character is unharmed after the action has been inflicted.

6. Comic Mischief—Depictions or dialogue involving slapstick or suggestive humor.

7. Crude Humor—Depictions or dialogue involving vulgar antics, including "bathroom" humor.

8. Drug Reference—Reference to and/or images of illegal drugs.

9. Fantasy Violence—Violent actions of a fantasy nature, involving human or non-human characters in situations easily distinguishable from real life.

10. Violence—Graphic and realistic-looking depictions of physical conflict. May involve extreme and/or realistic blood, gore, weapons and depictions of human injury and death.

11. Language—Mild to moderate use of profanity.

12. Lyrics—Mild references to profanity, sexuality, violence, alcohol or drug use in music.

13. Mature Humor—Depictions or dialogue involving "adult" humor, including sexual references.

14. Nudity—Graphic or prolonged depictions of nudity.

15. Partial Nudity—Brief and/or mild depictions of nudity.

16. Real Gambling—Player can gamble, including betting or wagering real cash or currency.

17. Sexual Content—Non-explicit depictions of sexual behavior, possibly including partial nudity.

18. Sexual Themes—References to sex or sexuality.

19. Sexual Violence—Depictions of rape or other violent sexual acts.

20. Simulated Gambling—Player can gamble without betting or wagering real cash or currency.

21. Strong Language—Explicit and/or frequent use of profanity.

22. Strong Lyrics—Explicit and/or frequent references to profanity, sex, violence, alcohol or drug use in music.

23. Strong Sexual Content—Explicit and/or frequent depictions of sexual behavior, possibly including nudity.

24. Suggestive Themes—Mild provocative references or materials.

25. Tobacco Reference—Reference to and/or images of tobacco products.

26. Use of Drugs—The consumption or use of illegal drugs.

27. Use of Alcohol—The consumption of alcoholic beverages.

28. Use of Tobacco—The consumption of tobacco products.

29. Violence—Scenes involving aggressive conflict. May contain bloodless dismemberment.

30. Violent References—References to violent acts.

In addition, when a content descriptor is preceded by the term "Mild," it is intended to convey low frequency, intensity, or severity of the content it modifies.

Online Gaming

The ESRB rating system only addresses the content created by the game publisher. It does not consider any content that may be created by individual players when they are playing ESRB-rated games that can be played online with other players.

However, ESRB-rated online games are required to display an Online Rating Notice that warns about possible exposure to chat or other types of user-generated content that have not been considered in rating the game. The Online Rating Notice appears on the game's packaging and on the opening screen, and states: "Online Interactions Not Rated by the ESRB."

Video Game Retailers

The ESRB is not authorized to enforce the rating system against video game retailers, however, many major retailers and chains have voluntarily implemented policies requiring age verification for the sale or rental of M (Mature) and AO (Adults Only) rated games. A recent study by the U.S. Federal Trade Commission (FTC) found that national retailers enforced this policy 80% of the time.

In 2006, the ESRB Retail Council (ERC) was established to further the commitment of national retailers in the United States to support ESRB ratings. The ERC is committed to educating consumers about ESRB video game ratings and encouraging voluntary compliance with the age verification policy by video game retailers.

Proposed Legislation

As discussed above, the video game industry, including video game publishers and retailers, generally adheres to a voluntary system of regulation and rating. Nevertheless, there are a number of legislative efforts presently pending that seek to regulate the content of video games:

1. The Video Games Rating Enforcement Act (S2215)—This proposed Act requires ratings labels on video games and prohibit sales and rentals of Mature (M) and Adults Only (AO) rated video games to minors.

2. The Truth in Video Game Rating Act (S568)—This proposed Act prohibits any rating organization from assigning a content rating to any video or computer game unless it has reviewed its entire playable content; prohibits any producer, seller, or distributor of such games from withholding or hiding any such content from a rating organization; requires any person submitting to a rating organization a video or computer game with hidden content to accompany it with the codes or methods necessary to access such hidden content; and prohibits a rating organization from providing a content rating that grossly mischaracterizes the game content.

3. The Video Game Decency Act of 2007 (HR1531)—This proposed Act makes it unlawful for any person to distribute any video game whose label contains an age-based content rating if, with the intent of obtaining a less restrictive age-based rating, that person fails to disclose game content to an independent ratings organization, with the result that the video game receives a less-restrictive age-based content rating; treats any violation as an unfair or deceptive act or practice; and preempts state or local law or regulation related to video game content rating.

4. The Children Protection from Video Game Violence and Sexual Content Act (HR2958)—This proposed Act requires the Federal Communications Commission (FCC) to study and report to Congress on the system employed by the Entertainment Software Ratings Board to assign ratings to video games, including the FCC's opinion on whether the system exposes children to excessive violence and sexual content; requires the Comptroller General to study and report to Congress on the impact of video games on the mental stability and growth of children and young adults.

5. The Parents' Empowerment Act (HR3899)—This proposed Act authorizes a minor, through a person acting on his or her behalf

under the Federal Rules of Civil Procedure, to bring a civil action in U.S. District Court for compensatory and punitive damages for the knowing sale or distribution of an entertainment product containing material harmful to minors, if: (1) a reasonable person would expect a substantial number of minors to be exposed to the material; and (2) the minor as a result of such exposure is likely to suffer personal or emotional injury or injury to mental or moral welfare. The bill would create an affirmative defense to such an action that: (1) a parent or guardian of the minor owned or possessed the entertainment product containing the material to which the minor was exposed; and (2) an act of that parent or guardian was the proximate cause of the minor's exposure.

6. The Video Games Rating Enforcement Act (HR5990)—This proposed Act requires ratings labels on video games and prohibits sales and rentals of M and AO rated video games to minors.

In addition to the proposed federal legislation, a number of states are considering similar legislation.

PAUSE PARENT PLAY

"Pause Parent Play" is a campaign designed to empower parents to choose what their children watch, hear and play, including movies, television, music, and video games. This coalition of corporations, entertainment companies and family groups, supported by members of Congress, are encouraging parents to:

1. Pause—Take a minute and think about how children might react to TV, movies, video games, or music;

2. Parent—Decide what is appropriate and talk with children about what media is right for them; and

3. Play—Enjoy media as a family.

The Pause Parent Play campaign gathers information from the various ratings systems devised by the movie, television, music, and video game industries. Their mission is to provide parents and caregivers easy-to-use resources in order to educate them to the content of various forms of media to which children may be exposed.

APPENDIX 1:
MILLER V. CALIFORNIA
[413 U.S. 15 (1973)]

MILLER v. CALIFORNIA, 413 U.S. 15 (1973), 93 S.Ct. 2607

APPEAL FROM THE APPELLATE DEPARTMENT, SUPERIOR COURT OF CALIFORNIA, COUNTY OF ORANGE

No. 70–73.

Argued January 18–19, 1972

Reargued November 7, 1972

Decided June 21, 1973

Appellant was convicted of mailing unsolicited sexually explicit material in violation of a California statute that approximately incorporated the obscenity test formulated in Memoirs v. Massachusetts, 383 U.S. 413, 418 (plurality opinion). The trial court instructed the jury to evaluate the materials by the contemporary community standards of California. Appellant's conviction was affirmed on appeal. In lieu of the obscenity criteria enunciated by the Memoirs plurality, it is held:

1. Obscene material is not protected by the First Amendment, Roth v. United States, 354 U.S. 476, reaffirmed. A work may be subject to state regulation where that work, taken as a whole, appeals to the prurient interest in sex; portrays, in a patently offensive way, sexual conduct specifically defined by the applicable state law; and, taken as a whole, does not have serious literary, artistic, political, or scientific value.

2. The basic guidelines for the trier of fact must be: (a) whether "the average person, applying contemporary community standards"

would find that the work, taken as a whole, appeals to the prurient interest, Roth, supra, at 489, (b) whether the work depicts or describes, in a patently offensive way, sexual conduct specifically defined by the applicable state law, and (c) whether the work, taken as a whole, lacks serious literary, artistic, political, or scientific value. If a state obscenity law is thus limited, First Amendment values are adequately protected by ultimate independent appellate review of constitutional claims when necessary.

3. The test of "utterly without redeeming social value" articulated in Memoirs, supra, is rejected as a constitutional standard.

4. The jury may measure the essentially factual issues of prurient appeal and patent offensiveness by the standard that prevails in the forum community, and need not employ a "national standard."

Vacated and remanded.

MR. CHIEF JUSTICE BURGER delivered the opinion of the Court.

This is one of a group of "obscenity-pornography" cases being reviewed by the Court in a re-examination of standards enunciated in earlier cases involving what Mr. Justice Harlan called "the intractable obscenity problem." Interstate Circuit, Inc. v. Dallas, 390 U.S. 676, 704 (1968) (concurring and dissenting).

Appellant conducted a mass mailing campaign to advertise the sale of illustrated books, euphemistically called "adult" material. After a jury trial, he was convicted of violating California Penal Code § 311.2(a), a misdemeanor, by knowingly distributing obscene matter, and the Appellate Department, Superior Court of California, County of Orange, summarily affirmed the judgment without opinion. Appellant's conviction was specifically based on his conduct in causing five unsolicited advertising brochures to be sent through the mail in an envelope addressed to a restaurant in Newport Beach, California. The envelope was opened by the manager of the restaurant and his mother. They had not requested the brochures; they complained to the police.

The brochures advertise four books entitled "Intercourse," "Man-Woman," "Sex Orgies Illustrated," and "An Illustrated History of Pornography," and a film entitled "Marital Intercourse." While the brochures contain some descriptive printed material, primarily they consist of pictures and drawings very explicitly depicting men and women in groups of two or more engaging in a variety of sexual activities, with genitals often prominently displayed.

I

This case involves the application of a State's criminal obscenity statute to a situation in which sexually explicit materials have been thrust by aggressive sales action upon unwilling recipients who had in no way indicated any desire to receive such materials. This Court has recognized that the States have a legitimate interest in prohibiting dissemination or exhibition of obscene material when the mode of dissemination carries with it a significant danger of offending the sensibilities of unwilling recipients or of exposure to juveniles. Stanley v. Georgia, 394 U.S. 557, 567 (1969); Ginsberg v. New York, 390 U.S. 629, 637–643 (1968); Interstate Circuit, Inc. v. Dallas, supra, at 690; Redrup v. New York, 386 U.S. 767, 769 (1967); Jacobellis v. Ohio, 378 U.S. 184, 195 (1964). See Rabe v. Washington, 405 U.S. 313, 317 (1972) (BURGER, C. J., concurring); United States v. Reidel, 402 U.S. 351, 360–362 (1971) (opinion of MARSHALL, J.); Joseph Burstyn, Inc. v. Wilson, 343 U.S. 495, 502 (1952); Breard v. Alexandria, 341 U.S. 622, 644–645 (1951); Kovacs v. Cooper, 336 U.S. 77, 88–89 (1949); Prince v. Massachusetts, 321 U.S. 158, 169–170 (1944). Cf. Butler v. Michigan, 352 U.S. 380, 382–383 (1957); Public Utilities Comm'n v. Pollak, 343 U.S. 451, 464–465 (1952). It is in this context that we are called on to define the standards which must be used to identify obscene material that a State may regulate without infringing on the First Amendment as applicable to the States through the Fourteenth Amendment.

The dissent of MR. JUSTICE BRENNAN review the background of the obscenity problem, but since the Court now undertakes to formulate standards more concrete than those in the past, it is useful for us to focus on two of the landmark cases in the somewhat tortured history of the Court's obscenity decisions. In Roth v. United States, 354 U.S. 476 (1957), the Court sustained a conviction under a federal statute punishing the mailing of "obscene, lewd, lascivious or filthy . . ." materials. The key to that holding was the Court's rejection of the claim that obscene materials were protected by the First Amendment. Five Justices joined in the opinion stating:

> "All ideas having even the slightest redeeming social importance—unorthodox ideas, controversial ideas, even ideas hateful to the prevailing climate of opinion—have the full protection of the [First Amendment] guaranties, unless excludable because they encroach upon the limited area of more important interests. But implicit in the history of the First Amendment is the rejection of obscenity as utterly without redeeming social importance. . . . This is the same judgment expressed by this Court in Chaplinsky v. New Hampshire, 315 U.S. 568, 571–572:
>
> > "' . . . There are certain well-defined and narrowly limited classes of speech, the prevention and punishment of which have never been thought to raise

any Constitutional problem. These include the lewd and obscene. . . . It has been well observed that such utterances are no essential part of any exposition of ideas, and are of such slight social value as a step to truth that any benefit that may be derived from them is clearly outweighed by the social interest in order and morality. . . .' [Emphasis by Court in Roth opinion.]

"We hold that obscenity is not within the area of constitutionally protected speech or press." 354 U.S., at 484–485 (footnotes omitted).

Nine years later, in Memoirs v. Massachusetts, 383 U.S. 413 (1966), the Court veered sharply away from the Roth concept and, with only three Justices in the plurality opinion, articulated a new test of obscenity. The plurality held that under the Roth definition, "as elaborated in subsequent cases, three elements must coalesce: it must be established that (a) the dominant theme of the material taken as a whole appeals to a prurient interest in sex; (b) the material is patently offensive because it affronts contemporary community standards relating to the description or representation of sexual matters; and (c) the material is utterly without redeeming social value." Id., at 418.

The sharpness of the break with Roth, represented by the third element of the Memoirs test and emphasized by MR. JUSTICE WHITE'S dissent, id., at 460–462, was further underscored when the Memoirs plurality went on to state:

"The Supreme Judicial Court erred in holding that a book need not be 'unqualifiedly worthless before it can be deemed obscene.' A book cannot be proscribed unless it is found to be utterly without redeeming social value." Id., at 419 (emphasis in original).

While Roth presumed "obscenity" to be "utterly without redeeming social importance," Memoirs required that to prove obscenity it must be affirmatively established that the material is "utterly without redeeming social value." Thus, even as they repeated the words of Roth, the Memoirs plurality produced a drastically altered test that called on the prosecution to prove a negative, i.e., that the material was "utterly without redeeming social value"—a burden virtually impossible to discharge under our criminal standards of proof. Such considerations caused Mr. Justice Harlan to wonder if the "utterly without redeeming social value" test had any meaning at all. See Memoirs v. Massachusetts, id., at 459 (Harlan, J., dissenting). See also id., at 461 (WHITE, J., dissenting); United States v. Groner, 479 F.2d 577, 579–581 (CA5 1973).

Apart from the initial formulation in the Roth case, no majority of the Court has at any given time been able to agree on a standard to determine what constitutes obscene, pornographic material subject to regulation under the States' police power. See, e.g., Redrup v. New York,

386 U.S., at 770–771. We have seen "a variety of views among the members of the Court unmatched in any other course of constitutional adjudication." Interstate Circuit, Inc. v. Dallas, 390 U.S., at 704–705 (Harlan, J., concurring and dissenting). This is not remarkable, for in the area of freedom of speech and press the courts must always remain sensitive to any infringement on genuinely serious literary, artistic, political, or scientific expression. This is an area in which there are few eternal verities.

The case we now review was tried on the theory that the California Penal Code § 311 approximately incorporates the three-stage Memoirs test, supra. But now the Memoirs test has been abandoned as unworkable by its author, and no Member of the Court today supports the Memoirs formulation.

II

This much has been categorically settled by the Court, that obscene material is unprotected by the First Amendment. Kois v. Wisconsin, 408 U.S. 229 (1972); United States v. Reidel, 402 U.S., at 354; Roth v. United States, supra, at 485. "The First and Fourteenth Amendments have never been treated as absolutes [footnote omitted]." Breard v. Alexandria, 341 U.S., at 642, and cases cited. See Times Film Corp. v. Chicago, 365 U.S. 43, 47–50 (1961); Joseph Burstyn, Inc. v. Wilson, 343 U.S., at 502. We acknowledge, however, the inherent dangers of undertaking to regulate any form of expression. State statutes designed to regulate obscene materials must be carefully limited. See Interstate Circuit, Inc. v. Dallas, supra, at 682–685. As a result, we now confine the permissible scope of such regulation to works which depict or describe sexual conduct. That conduct must be specifically defined by the applicable state law, as written or authoritatively construed. A state offense must also be limited to works which, taken as a whole, appeal to the prurient interest in sex, which portray sexual conduct in a patently offensive way, and which, taken as a whole, do not have serious literary, artistic, political, or scientific value.

The basic guidelines for the trier of fact must be: (a) whether "the average person, applying contemporary community standards" would find that the work, taken as a whole, appeals to the prurient interest, Kois v. Wisconsin, supra, at 230, quoting Roth v. United States, supra, at 489; (b) whether the work depicts or describes, in a patently offensive way, sexual conduct specifically defined by the applicable state law; and (c) whether the work, taken as a whole, lacks serious literary, artistic, political, or scientific value. We do not adopt as a constitutional standard the "utterly without redeeming social value" test of Memoirs v. Massachusetts, 383 U.S., at 419; that concept has never commanded the adherence of more than three Justices at one time. See supra, at 21. If a state law that regulates obscene material is thus limited, as written or construed, the First Amendment values applicable to the States through the Fourteenth Amendment are adequately protected by the ultimate power of appellate courts to conduct an independent review of constitutional claims when necessary. See Kois v. Wisconsin, supra, at 232; Memoirs v. Massachusetts, supra, at 459–460 (Harlan, J., dissenting); Jacobellis v. Ohio, 378 U.S., at 204 (Harlan, J., dissenting); New York Times Co. v. Sullivan, 376 U.S. 254, 284–285 (1964); Roth v. United States, supra, at 497–498 (Harlan, J., concurring and dissenting).

We emphasize that it is not our function to propose regulatory schemes for the States. That must await their concrete legislative efforts. It is possible, however, to give a few plain examples of what a state statute could define for regulation under part (b) of the standard announced in this opinion, supra:

(a) Patently offensive representations or descriptions of ultimate sexual acts, normal or perverted, actual or simulated.

(b) Patently offensive representations or descriptions of masturbation, excretory functions, and lewd exhibition of the genitals.

Sex and nudity may not be exploited without limit by films or pictures exhibited or sold in places of public accommodation any more than live sex and nudity can be exhibited or sold without limit in such public places. At a minimum, prurient, patently offensive depiction or description of sexual conduct must have serious literary, artistic, political, or scientific value to merit First Amendment protection. See Kois v. Wisconsin, supra, at 230–232; Roth v. United States, supra, at 487; Thornhill v. Alabama, 310 U.S. 88, 101–102 (1940). For example, medical books for the education of physicians and related personnel necessarily use graphic illustrations and descriptions of human anatomy. In resolving the inevitably sensitive questions of fact and law, we must continue to rely on the jury system, accompanied by the safeguards that judges, rules of evidence, presumption of innocence, and other protective features provide, as we do with rape, murder, and a host of other offenses against society and its individual members.

MR. JUSTICE BRENNAN, author of the opinions of the Court, or the plurality opinions, in Roth v. United States, supra; Jacobellis v. Ohio, supra; Ginzburg v. United States, 383 U.S. 463 (1966), Mishkin v. New York, 383 U.S. 502 (1966); and Memoirs v. Massachusetts, supra, has abandoned his former position and now maintains that no formulation of this Court, the Congress, or the States can adequately distinguish obscene material unprotected by the First Amendment from protected expression, Paris Adult Theatre I v. Slaton, post, p. 73 (BRENNAN, J., dissenting). Paradoxically, MR. JUSTICE BRENNAN indicates that suppression of unprotected obscene material is permissible to avoid exposure to unconsenting adults, as in this case, and to juveniles, although he gives no indication of how the division between protected and nonprotected materials may be drawn with greater precision for these purposes than for regulation of commercial exposure to consenting adults only. Nor does he indicate where in the Constitution he finds the authority to distinguish between a willing "adult" one month past the state law age of majority and a willing "juvenile" one month younger.

Under the holdings announced today, no one will be subject to prosecution for the sale or exposure of obscene materials unless these materials depict or describe patently offensive "hard core" sexual conduct specifically defined by the regulating state law, as written or construed. We are satisfied that these specific prerequisites will provide fair notice to a dealer in such materials that his public and commercial activities may bring prosecution. See Roth v. United States, supra, at 491–492. Cf. Ginsberg v. New York, 390 U.S., at 643. If the inability to define regulated materials with ultimate, god-like precision altogether removes the power of the States or the Congress to regulate, then "hard core" pornography may be exposed without limit to the juvenile, the passerby, and the consenting adult alike, as, indeed, MR. JUSTICE DOUGLAS contends. As to MR. JUSTICE DOUGLAS' position, see United States v. Thirty-seven Photographs, 402 U.S. 363, 379–380 (1971) (Black, J., joined by DOUGLAS, J., dissenting); Ginzburg v. United States, supra, at 476, 491–492 (Black, J., and DOUGLAS, J., dissenting); Jacobellis v. Ohio, supra, at 196 (Black, J., joined by DOUGLAS, J., concurring); Roth, supra, at 508–514 (DOUGLAS, J., dissenting). In this belief, however,

MR. JUSTICE DOUGLAS now stands alone.

MR. JUSTICE BRENNAN also emphasizes "institutional stress" in justification of his change of view. Noting that "[t]he number of obscenity cases on our docket gives ample testimony to the burden that has been placed upon this Court," he quite rightly remarks that the examination of contested materials "is hardly a source of edification to the members of this Court." Paris Adult Theatre I v. Slaton, post, at 92, 93. He also notes, and we agree, that "uncertainty of the standards creates a continuing source of tension between state and federal courts. . . ." "The problem is . . . that one cannot say with certainty that material is obscene until at least five members of this Court, applying inevitably obscure standards, have pronounced it so." Id., at 93, 92.

It is certainly true that the absence, since Roth, of a single majority view of this Court as to proper standards for testing obscenity has placed a strain on both state and federal courts. But today, for the first time since Roth was decided in 1957, a majority of this Court has agreed on concrete guidelines to isolate "hard core" pornography from expression protected by the First Amendment. Now we may abandon the casual practice of Redrup v. New York, 386 U.S. 767 (1967), and attempt to provide positive guidance to federal and state courts alike.

This may not be an easy road, free from difficulty. But no amount of "fatigue" should lead us to adopt a convenient "institutional" rationale— an absolutist, "anything goes" view of the First Amendment—because it will lighten our burdens. "Such an abnegation of judicial supervision in this field would be inconsistent with our duty to uphold the constitutional guarantees." Jacobellis v. Ohio, supra, at 187–188 (opinion of BRENNAN, J.). Nor should we remedy "tension between state and federal courts" by arbitrarily depriving the States of a power reserved to them under the Constitution, a power which they have enjoyed and exercised continuously from before the adoption of the First Amendment to this day. See Roth v. United States, supra, at 482–485. "Our duty admits of no 'substitute for facing up to the tough individual problems of constitutional judgment involved in every obscenity case.' [Roth v. United States, supra, at 498]; see Manual Enterprises, Inc. v. Day, 370 U.S. 478, 488 (opinion of Harlan, J.) [footnote omitted]." Jacobellis v. Ohio, supra, at 188 (opinion of BRENNAN, J.).

III

Under a National Constitution, fundamental First Amendment limitations on the powers of the States do not vary from community to community, but this does not mean that there are, or should or can be, fixed, uniform national standards of precisely what appeals to the "prurient interest" or is "patently offensive." These are essentially questions of fact, and our Nation is simply too big and too diverse for this Court to reasonably expect that such standards could be articulated for all 50 States in a single formulation, even assuming the prerequisite consensus exists. When triers of fact are asked to decide whether "the average person, applying contemporary community standards" would consider certain materials "prurient," it would be unrealistic to require that the answer be based on some abstract formulation. The adversary system, with lay jurors as the usual ultimate factfinders in criminal prosecutions, has historically permitted triers of fact to draw on the standards of their community, guided always by limiting instructions on the law. To require a State to structure obscenity proceedings around evidence of a national "community standard" would be an exercise in futility.

As noted before, this case was tried on the theory that the California obscenity statute sought to incorporate the tripartite test of Memoirs. This, a "national" standard of First Amendment protection enumerated by a plurality of this Court, was correctly regarded at the time of trial as limiting state prosecution under the controlling case law. The jury, however, was explicitly instructed that, in determining whether the "dominant theme of the material as a whole . . . appeals to the prurient interest" and in determining whether the material "goes substantially beyond customary limits of candor and affronts contemporary community standards of decency," it was to apply "contemporary community standards of the State of California."

During the trial, both the prosecution and the defense assumed that the relevant "community standards" in making the factual determination of obscenity were those of the State of California, not some hypothetical standard of the entire United States of America. Defense counsel at trial never objected to the testimony of the State's expert on community standards or to the instructions of the trial judge on "statewide" standards. On appeal to the Appellate Department, Superior Court of California, County of Orange, appellant for the first time contended that application of state, rather than national, standards violated the First and Fourteenth Amendments.

We conclude that neither the State's alleged failure to offer evidence of "national standards," nor the trial court's charge that the jury consider state community standards, were constitutional errors. Nothing in the First Amendment requires that a jury must consider hypothetical and unascertainable "national standards" when attempting to determine whether certain materials are obscene as a matter of fact. Mr. Chief Justice Warren pointedly commented in his dissent in Jacobellis v. Ohio, supra, at 200:

> "It is my belief that when the Court said in Roth that obscenity is to be defined by reference to 'community standards,' it meant community standards— not a national standard, as is sometimes argued. I believe that there is no provable 'national standard.' . . . At all events, this Court has not been able to enunciate one, and it would be unreasonable to expect local courts to divine one."

It is neither realistic nor constitutionally sound to read the First Amendment as requiring that the people of Maine or Mississippi accept public depiction of conduct found tolerable in Las Vegas, or New York City. See Hoyt v. Minnesota, 399 U.S. 524–525 (1970) (BLACKMUN, J., dissenting); Walker v. Ohio, 398 U.S. 434 (1970) (BURGER, C. J., dissenting); id., at 434–435 (Harlan, J., dissenting); Cain v. Kentucky, 397 U.S. 319 (1970) (BURGER, C. J., dissenting); id., at 319–320 (Harlan, J., dissenting); United States v. Groner, 479 F.2d, at 581–583; O'Meara & Shaffer, Obscenity in The Supreme Court: A Note on Jacobellis v. Ohio, 40 Notre Dame Law. 1, 6–7 (1964). See also Memoirs v. Massachusetts, 383 U.S., at 458 (Harlan, J., dissenting); Jacobellis v. Ohio, supra, at 203–204 (Harlan, J., dissenting); Roth v. United States, supra, at 505–506 (Harlan, J., concurring and dissenting). People in different States vary in their tastes and attitudes, and this diversity is not to be strangled by the absolutism of imposed uniformity. As the Court made clear in Mishkin v. New York, 383 U.S., at 508–509, the primary concern with requiring a jury to apply the standard of "the average person, applying contemporary community standards" is to be certain that, so far as material is not aimed at a deviant group, it will be judged by its impact on an average person, rather than a particularly susceptible or sensitive person—or indeed a totally insensitive one. See Roth v. United States, supra, at 489. Cf. the now discredited test in Regina v. Hicklin, [1868] L. R. 3 Q. B. 360. We hold that the requirement that the jury evaluate the materials with reference to "contemporary standards of the State of California" serves this protective purpose and is constitutionally adequate.

IV

The dissenting Justices sound the alarm of repression. But, in our view, to equate the free and robust exchange of ideas and political debate with commercial exploitation of obscene material demeans the grand conception of the First Amendment and its high purposes in the historic struggle for freedom. It is a "misuse of the great guarantees of free speech and free press. . . ." Breard v. Alexandria, 341 U.S., at 645. The First Amendment protects works which, taken as a whole, have serious literary, artistic, political, or scientific value, regardless of whether the government or a majority of the people approve of the ideas these works represent. "The protection given speech and press was fashioned to assure unfettered interchange of ideas for the bringing about of political and social changes desired by the people," Roth v. United States, supra, at 484 (emphasis added). See Kois v. Wisconsin, 408 U.S., at 230–232; Thornhill v. Alabama, 310 U.S., at 101–102. But the public portrayal of hard-core sexual conduct for its own sake, and for the ensuing commercial gain, is a different matter.

There is no evidence, empirical or historical, that the stern 19th century American censorship of public distribution and display of material relating to sex, see Roth v. United States, supra, at 482–485, in any way limited or affected expression of serious literary, artistic, political, or scientific ideas. On the contrary, it is beyond any question that the era following Thomas Jefferson to Theodore Roosevelt was an "extraordinarily vigorous period," not just in economics and politics, but in belles lettres and in "the outlying fields of social and political philosophies." We do not see the harsh hand of censorship of ideas—good or bad, sound or unsound—and "repression" of political liberty lurking in every state regulation of commercial exploitation of human interest in sex.

MR. JUSTICE BRENNAN finds "it is hard to see how state-ordered regimentation of our minds can ever be forestalled." Paris Adult Theatre I v. Slaton, post, at 110 (BRENNAN, J., dissenting). These doleful anticipations assume that courts cannot distinguish commerce in ideas, protected by the First Amendment, from commercial exploitation of obscene material. Moreover, state regulation of hard-core pornography so as to make it unavailable to nonadults, a regulation which MR. JUSTICE BRENNAN finds constitutionally permissible, has all the elements of "censorship" for adults; indeed even more rigid enforcement techniques may be called for with such dichotomy of regulation. See Interstate Circuit, Inc. v. Dallas, 390 U.S., at 690. One can concede that the "sexual revolution" of recent years may have had useful byproducts in striking layers of prudery from a subject long irrationally kept from needed ventilation. But it does not follow that no regulation of patently offensive "hard core" materials is needed or permissible; civilized people do not allow unregulated access to heroin because it is a derivative of medicinal morphine.

In sum, we (a) reaffirm the Roth holding that obscene material is not protected by the First Amendment; (b) hold that such material can be regulated by the States, subject to the specific safeguards enunciated above, without a showing that the material is "utterly without redeeming social value"; and (c) hold that obscenity is to be determined by applying "contemporary community standards," see Kois v. Wisconsin, supra, at 230, and Roth v. United States, supra, at 489, not "national standards." The judgment of the Appellate Department of the Superior Court, Orange County, California, is vacated and the case remanded to that court for further proceedings not inconsistent with the First

Amendment standards established by this opinion. See United States v. 12 200-ft. Reels of Film, post, at 130 n. 7.

Vacated and remanded.

MR. JUSTICE DOUGLAS, dissenting.

***

I

Today we leave open the way for California to send a man to prison for distributing brochures that advertise books and a movie under freshly written standards defining obscenity which until today's decision were never the part of any law.

The Court has worked hard to define obscenity and concededly has failed. In Roth v. United States, 354 U.S. 476, it ruled that "[o]bscene material is material which deals with sex in a manner appealing to prurient interest." Id., at 487. Obscenity, it was said, was rejected by the First Amendment because it is "utterly without redeeming social importance." Id., at 484. The presence of a "prurient interest" was to be determined by "contemporary community standards." Id., at 489. That test, it has been said, could not be determined by one standard here and another standard there, Jacobellis v. Ohio, 378 U.S. 184, 194, but "on the basis of a national standard." Id., at 195. My Brother STEWART in Jacobellis commented that the difficulty of the Court in giving content to obscenity was that it was "faced with the task of trying to define what may be indefinable." Id., at 197.

In Memoirs v. Massachusetts, 383 U.S. 413, 418, the Roth test was elaborated to read as follows: "[T]hree elements must coalesce: it must be established that (a) the dominant theme of the material taken as a whole appeals to a prurient interest in sex; (b) the material is patently offensive because it affronts contemporary community standards relating to the description or representation of sexual matters; and (c) the material is utterly without redeeming social value."

In Ginzburg v. United States, 383 U.S. 463, a publisher was sent to prison, not for the kind of books and periodicals he sold, but for the manner in which the publications were advertised. The "leer of the sensualist" was said to permeate the advertisements. Id., at 468. The Court said, "Where the purveyor's sole emphasis is on the sexually provocative aspects of his publications, that fact may be decisive in the determination of obscenity." Id., at 470. As Mr. Justice Black said in dissent, " . . . Ginzburg . . . is now finally and authoritatively condemned to serve five years in prison for distributing printed matter about sex which neither Ginzburg nor anyone else could possibly have known to be criminal." Id., at 476. That observation by Mr. Justice Black is underlined by the fact that the Ginzburg decision was five to four.

A further refinement was added by Ginsberg v. New York, 390 U.S. 629, 641, where the Court held that "it was not irrational for the legislature to find that exposure to material condemned by the statute is harmful to minors."

But even those members of this Court who had created the new and changing standards of "obscenity" could not agree on their application. And so we adopted a per curiam treatment of so-called obscene publications that seemed to pass constitutional muster under the several constitutional tests which had been formulated. See Redrup v. New York, 386 U.S. 767. Some condemn it if its "dominant tendency might be to 'deprave or corrupt' a reader." Others look not to the content of the book but to whether it is advertised "'to appeal to the erotic interests of customers.' " Some condemn only "hardcore pornography"; but even then a true definition is lacking. It has indeed been said of that definition, "I could never succeed in [defining it] intelligibly," but "I know it when I see it."

Today we would add a new three-pronged test:

> "(a) whether 'the average person, applying contemporary community standards' would find that the work, taken as a whole, appeals to the prurient interest, . . . (b) whether the work depicts or describes, in a patently offensive way, sexual conduct specifically defined by the applicable state law, and (c) whether the work, taken as a whole, lacks serious literary, artistic, political, or scientific value."

Those are the standards we ourselves have written into the Constitution. Yet how under these vague tests can we sustain convictions for the sale of an article prior to the time when some court has declared it to be obscene?

Today the Court retreats from the earlier formulations of the constitutional test and undertakes to make new definitions. This effort, like the earlier ones, is earnest and well intentioned. The difficulty is that we do not deal with constitutional terms, since "obscenity" is not mentioned in the Constitution or Bill of Rights. And the First Amendment makes no such exception from "the press" which it undertakes to protect nor, as I have said on other occasions, is an exception necessarily implied, for there was no recognized exception to the free press at the time the Bill of Rights was adopted which treated "obscene" publications differently from other types of papers, magazines, and books. So there are no constitutional guidelines for deciding what is and what is not "obscene." The Court is at large because we deal with tastes and standards of literature.

What shocks me may be sustenance for my neighbor. What causes one person to boil up in rage over one pamphlet or movie may reflect only his neurosis, not shared by others. We deal here with a regime of censorship which, if adopted, should be done by constitutional amendment after full debate by the people.

Obscenity cases usually generate tremendous emotional outbursts. They have no business being in the courts. If a constitutional amendment authorized censorship, the censor would probably be an administrative agency. Then criminal prosecutions could follow as, if, and when publishers defied the censor and sold their literature. Under that regime a publisher would know when he was on dangerous ground. Under the present regime—whether the old standards or the new ones are used—the criminal law becomes a trap. A brand new test would put a publisher behind bars under a new law improvised by the courts after the publication. That was done in Ginzburg and has all the evils of an ex post facto law.

My contention is that until a civil proceeding has placed a tract beyond the pale, no criminal prosecution should be sustained. For no more vivid illustration of vague and uncertain laws could be designed than those we have fashioned. As Mr. Justice Harlan has said:

> "The upshot of all this divergence in viewpoint is that anyone who undertakes to examine the Court's decisions since Roth which have held particular material obscene or not obscene would find himself in utter bewilderment." Interstate Circuit, Inc. v. Dallas, 390 U.S. 676, 707.

In Bouie v. City of Columbia, 378 U.S. 347, we upset a conviction for remaining on property after being asked to leave, while the only unlawful act charged by the statute was entering. We held that the defendants had received no "fair warning, at the time of their conduct" while on the property "that the act for which they now stand convicted was rendered criminal" by the state statute. Id., at 355. The same requirement of "fair warning" is due here, as much as in Bouie. The latter involved racial discrimination; the present case involves rights earnestly urged as being protected by the First Amendment. In any case—certainly when constitutional rights are concerned—we should not allow men to go to prison or be fined when they had no "fair warning" that what they did was criminal conduct.

II

If a specific book, play, paper, or motion picture has in a civil proceeding been condemned as obscene and review of that finding has been completed, and thereafter a person publishes, shows, or displays that particular book or film, then a vague law has been made specific. There would remain the underlying question whether the First Amendment allows an implied exception in the case of obscenity. I do not think it does and my views on the issue have been stated over and over again. But at least a criminal prosecution brought at that juncture would not violate the time-honored void-for-vagueness test.

No such protective procedure has been designed by California in this case. Obscenity—which even we cannot define with precision—is a hodge-podge. To send men to jail for violating standards they cannot understand, construe, and apply is a monstrous thing to do in a Nation dedicated to fair trials and due process.

III

While the right to know is the corollary of the right to speak or publish, no one can be forced by government to listen to disclosure that he finds offensive. That was the basis of my dissent in Public Utilities Comm'n v. Pollak, 343 U.S. 451, 467, where I protested against making streetcar passengers a "captive" audience. There is no "captive audience" problem in these obscenity cases. No one is being compelled to look or to listen. Those who enter newsstands or bookstalls may be offended by what they see. But they are not compelled by the State to frequent those places; and it is only state or governmental action against which the First Amendment, applicable to the States by virtue of the Fourteenth, raises a ban.

The idea that the First Amendment permits government to ban publications that are "offensive" to some people puts an ominous gloss on freedom of the press. That test would make it possible to ban any paper or any journal or magazine in some benighted place. The First Amendment was designed "to invite dispute," to induce "a condition of unrest," to "create dissatisfaction with conditions as they are," and even to stir "people to anger." Terminiello v. Chicago, 337 U.S. 1, 4. The idea that the First Amendment permits punishment for ideas that are "offensive" to the particular judge or jury sitting in judgment is astounding. No greater leveler of speech or literature has ever been designed. To give the power to the censor, as we do today, is to make a sharp and radical break with the traditions of a free society. The First Amendment was not fashioned as a vehicle for dispensing tranquilizers to the people. Its prime function was to keep debate open to "offensive" as well as to "staid" people. The tendency throughout history has been to subdue the individual and to exalt the power of government. The use of the standard "offensive" gives authority to government that cuts the very vitals out of the First Amendment. As is intimated by the Court's opinion, the materials before us may be garbage. But so is much of what is said in political campaigns, in the daily press, on TV, or over the radio. By reason of the First Amendment—and solely because of it-speakers and publishers have not been threatened or subdued because their thoughts and ideas may be "offensive" to some.

The standard "offensive" is unconstitutional in yet another way. In Coates v. City of Cincinnati, 402 U.S. 611, we had before us a municipal ordinance that made it a crime for three or more persons to assemble on a street and conduct themselves "in a manner annoying to persons passing by." We struck it down, saying: "If three or more people meet together on a sidewalk or street corner, they must conduct themselves so as not to annoy any police officer or other person who should happen to pass by. In our opinion this ordinance is unconstitutionally vague because it subjects the exercise of the right of assembly to an unascertainable standard, and unconstitutionally broad because it authorizes the punishment of constitutionally protected conduct.

> "Conduct that annoys some people does not annoy others. Thus, the ordinance is vague, not in the sense that it requires a person to conform his conduct to an imprecise but comprehensive normative standard, but rather in the sense that no standard of conduct is specified at all." Id., at 614.

How we can deny Ohio the convenience of punishing people who "annoy" others and allow California power to punish people who publish materials "offensive" to some people is difficult to square with constitutional requirements.

If there are to be restraints on what is obscene, then a constitutional amendment should be the way of achieving the end. There are societies where religion and mathematics are the only free segments. It would be a dark day for America if that were our destiny. But the people can make it such if they choose to write obscenity into the Constitution and define it.

We deal with highly emotional, not rational, questions. To many the Song of Solomon is obscene. I do not think we, the judges, were ever given the constitutional power to make definitions of obscenity. If it is to be defined, let the people debate and decide by a constitutional amendment what they want to ban as obscene and what standards they want the legislatures and the courts to apply. Perhaps the people will decide that the path towards a mature, integrated society requires that all ideas competing for acceptance must have no censor. Perhaps they will decide otherwise. Whatever the choice, the courts will have some guidelines. Now we have none except our own predilections.

MR. JUSTICE BRENNAN, with whom MR. JUSTICE STEWART and MR. JUSTICE MARSHALL join, dissenting.

In my dissent in Paris Adult Theatre I v. Slaton, post, p. 73, decided this date, I noted that I had no occasion to consider the extent of state power to regulate the distribution of sexually oriented material to juveniles or the offensive exposure of such material to unconsenting adults. In the case before us, appellant was convicted of distributing obscene matter in violation of California Penal Code § 311.2, on the basis of evidence that he had caused to be mailed unsolicited brochures advertising various books and a movie. I need not now decide whether a statute might be drawn to impose, within the requirements of the First Amendment, criminal penalties for the precise conduct at issue here. For it is clear that under my dissent in Paris Adult Theatre I, the statute under which the prosecution was brought is unconstitutionally overbroad, and therefore invalid on its face. "[T]he transcendent value to all society of constitutionally protected expression is deemed to justify allowing 'attacks on overly broad statutes with no requirement that the person making the attack demonstrate that his own conduct could not be regulated by a statute drawn with the requisite narrow specificity.'" Gooding v. Wilson, 405 U.S. 518, 521 (1972), quoting from Dombrowski v. Pfister, 380 U.S. 479, 486 (1965). See also Baggett v. Bullitt, 377 U.S. 360, 366 (1964); Coates v. City of Cincinnati, 402 U.S. 611, 616 (1971); id., at 619–620 (WHITE, J., dissenting); United States v. Raines, 362 U.S. 17, 21–22 (1960); NAACP v. Button, 371 U.S. 415, 433 (1963). Since my view in Paris Adult Theatre I represents a substantial departure from the course of our prior decisions, and since the state courts have as yet had no opportunity to consider whether a "readily apparent construction suggests itself as a vehicle for rehabilitating the [statute] in a single prosecution," Dombrowski v. Pfister, supra, at 491, I would reverse the judgment of the Appellate Department of the Superior Court and remand the case for proceedings not inconsistent with this opinion. See Coates v. City of Cincinnati, supra, at 616.

APPENDIX 2:
POPE V. ILLINOIS [481 U.S. 497 (1987)]

POPE v. ILLINOIS, 481 U.S. 497 (1987), 107 S.Ct. 1918

CERTIORARI TO THE APPELLATE COURT OF ILLINOIS, SECOND DISTRICT

No. 85–1973.

Argued February 24, 1987

Decided May 4, 1987

Under Miller v. California, 413 U.S. 15, the third or "value" prong of the tripartite test for judging whether material is obscene requires the trier of fact to determine "whether the work, taken as a whole, lacks serious literary, artistic, political, or scientific value." After petitioners, both of whom were attendants at adult bookstores, sold certain magazines to police, they were separately charged with the offense of "obscenity" under Illinois law. Both trial courts instructed the respective juries that, to convict, they must find, inter alia, that the magazines were without "value." The juries were also instructed to judge whether the material was obscene by determining how it would be viewed by ordinary adults in the whole State of Illinois. The State Appellate Court affirmed both petitioners' convictions, rejecting thei contention that the "value" issue must be determined solely on an objective basis and not by reference to "contemporary community standards."

Held:

1. In a prosecution for the sale of allegedly obscene materials, the jury should not be instructed to apply community standards in deciding the value question. Only the first and second prongs of the Miller

test—appeal to prurient interest and patent offensiveness—should be decided with reference to "contemporary community standards." The ideas that a work represents need not obtain majority approval to merit protection, and the value of that work does not vary from community to community based on the degree of local acceptance it has won. The proper inquiry is not whether an ordinary member of any given community would find serious value in the allegedly obscene material, but whether a reasonable person would find such value in the material, taken as a whole. The instruction at issue therefore violated the First and Fourteenth Amendments.

2. Whether petitioners' convictions should be reversed outrigh or are subject to salvage because the erroneous instruction constituted harmless error will not be decided by this Court, since the State Appellate Court has not considered the harmless-error issue. Under Rose v. Clark, 478 U.S. 570, in the absence of error that renders a trial fundamentally unfair, a conviction should be affirmed where the reviewing court can find that the record developed at trial established guilt beyond a reasonable doubt. Here, since the jurors were not precluded from considering the value question, petitioners' convictions should stand despite the erroneous "community standards" instruction if the appellate court concludes that no rational juror, if properly instructed, could find "value" in the magazines petitioners sold. 138 Ill. App.3d 726, 486 N.E.2d 350, vacated and remanded.

WHITE, J., delivered the opinion of the Court, in which REHNQUIST, C. J., and POWELL, O'CONNOR, and SCALIA, JJ., joined, and in Parts I and II of which BLACKMUN, J., joined. SCALIA, J., filed a concurring opinion, post, p. 504. BLACKMUN, J., filed an opinion concurring in part and dissenting in part, post, p. 505. BRENNAN, J., filed a dissenting opinion, post, p. 506. STEVENS, J., filed a dissenting opinion, in which MARSHALL, J., joined, in all but n. 11 of which BRENNAN, J., joined, and in Part I of which BLACKMUN, J., joined, post, p. 507.

JUSTICE WHITE delivered the opinion of the Court.

In Miller v. California, 413 U.S. 15 (1973), the Court set out a tripartite test for judging whether material is obscene. The third prong of the Miller test requires the trier of fact to determine "whether the work, taken as a whole, lacks serious literary, artistic, political, or scientific value." Id., at 24. The issue in this case is whether, in a prosecution for the sale of allegedly obscene materials, the jury may be instructed to apply community standards in deciding the value question.

I

On July 21, 1983, Rockford, Illinois, police detectives purchased certain magazines from the two petitioners, each of whom was an attendant at an adult bookstore. Petitioners were subsequently charged separately with the offense of "obscenity" for the sale of these magazines. Each petitioner moved to dismiss the charges against him on the ground that the then-current version of the Illinois obscenity statute, Ill. Rev. Stat., ch. 38, ¶ 11–20 (1983), violated the First and Fourteenth Amendments to the United States Constitution. Both petitioners argued, among other things, that the statute was unconstitutional in failing to require that the value question be judged "solely on an objective basis as opposed to reference [sic] to contemporary community standards." App. 8, 22. Both trial courts rejected this contention and instructed the respective juries to judge whether the material was obscene by determining how it would be viewed by ordinary adults in the whole State of Illinois. Both petitioners were found guilty, and both appealed to the Illinois Appellate Court, Second District. That court also rejected petitioners' contention that the issue of value must be determined on an objective basis and not by reference to contemporary community standards. 138 Ill. App.3d 726, 486 N.E.2d 350 (1985); 138 Ill. App.3d 595, 486 N.E.2d 345 (1985). The Illinois Supreme Court denied review, and we granted certiorari, 479 U.S. 812 (1986).

II

There is no suggestion in our cases that the question of the value of an allegedly obscene work is to be determined by reference to community standards. Indeed, our cases are to the contrary. Smith v. United States, 431 U.S. 291 (1977), held that, in a federal prosecution for mailing obscene materials, the first and second prongs of the Miller test— appeal to prurient interest and patent offensiveness—are issues of fact for the jury to determine applying contemporary community standards. The Court then observed that, unlike prurient appeal and patent offensiveness, "[l]iterary, artistic, political, or scientific value . . . is not discussed in Miller in terms of contemporary community standards." Id., at 301 (citing F. Schauer, The Law of Obscenity 123–124 (1976)). This comment was not meant to point out an oversight in the Miller opinion, but to call attention to and approve a deliberate choice. In Miller itself, the Court was careful to point out that "[t]he First Amendment protects works which, taken as a whole, have serious literary, artistic, political, or scientific value, regardless of whether the government or a majority of the people approve of the ideas these works represent." 413 U.S., at 34. Just as the ideas a work represents need not obtain majority approval to merit protection, neither, insofar as the First Amendment is concerned, does the value of the work vary from community to community based on the degree of local acceptance it has won. The proper inquiry is not whether an ordinary member of any given community would find serious literary, artistic, political, or scientific value in allegedly obscene material, but whether a reasonable person would find such value in the material, taken as a whole. The instruction at issue in this case was therefore unconstitutional.

III

The question remains whether the convictions should be reversed outright or are subject to salvage if the erroneous instruction is found to be harmless error. Petitioners contend that the statute is invalid on its face and that the convictions must necessarily be reversed because, as we understand it, the State should not be allowed to preserve any conviction under a law that poses a threat to First Amendment values. But the statute under which petitioners were convicted is no longer on the books; it has been repealed and replaced by a statute that does not call for the application of community standards to the value question. Facial invalidation of the repealed statute would not serve the purpose of preventing future prosecutions under a constitutionally defective standard. Cf., e. g., Secretary of State of Maryland v. Joseph H. Munson Co., 467 U.S. 947, 964–968, and n. 13 (1984). And if we did facially invalidate the repealed statute and reverse petitioners' convictions, petitioners could still be retried under that statute, provided that the erroneous instruction was not repeated, because petitioners could not plausibly claim that the repealed statute failed to give them notice that the sale of obscene materials would be prosecuted. See Dombrowski v. Pfister, 380 U.S. 479, 491, n. 7 (1965); United States v. Thirty-seven Photographs, 402 U.S. 363, 375, n. 3 (1971). Under these circumstances, we see no reason to require a retrial if it can be said beyond a reasonable doubt that the jury's verdict in this case was not affected by the erroneous instruction.

The situation here is comparable to that in Rose v. Clark, 478 U.S. 570 (1986). In Rose, the jury in a murder trial was incorrectly instructed on the element of malice, yet the Court held that a harmless-error inquiry was appropriate. The Court explained that in the absence of error that renders a trial fundamentally unfair, such as denial of the right to counsel or trial before a financially interested judge, a conviction should be affirmed "[w]here a reviewing court can find that the record developed at trial established guilt beyond a reasonable doubt. . . ." Id., at 579. The error in Rose did not entirely preclude the jury from considering the element of malice, id., at 580, n. 8, and the fact that the jury could conceivably have had the impermissible presumption in mind when it considered the element of malice was not a reason to retry the defendant if the facts that the jury necessarily found established guilt beyond a reasonable doubt. The Court said: "When a jury is instructed to presume malice from predicate facts, it still must find the existence of those facts beyond reasonable doubt. Connecticut v. Johnson, 460 U.S. 73, 96–97 (1983) (POWELL, J., dissenting). In many cases, the predicate facts conclusively establish intent, so that no rational jury could find that the defendant committed the relevant criminal act but did not intend to cause injury." Id., at 580–581.

Similarly, in the present cases the jurors were not precluded from considering the question of value: they were informed that to convict they must find, among other things, that the magazines petitioners sold were utterly without redeeming social value. While it was error to instruct the juries to use a state community standard in considering the value question, if a reviewing court concludes that no rational juror, if properly instructed, could find value in the magazines, the convictions should stand.

Although we plainly have the authority to decide whether, on the facts of a given case, a constitutional error was harmless under the standard of Chapman v. California, 386 U.S. 18 (1967), we do so sparingly. Rose v. Clark, supra, at 584. In this case the Illinois Appellate Court has not considered the harmless-error issue. We therefore vacate its judgment and remand so that it may do so.

It is so ordered.

JUSTICE SCALIA, concurring.

I join the Court's opinion with regard to harmless error because I think it implausible that a community standard embracing the entire State of Illinois would cause any jury to convict where a "reasonable person" standard would not. At least in these circumstances, if a reviewing court concludes that no rational juror, properly instructed, could find value in the magazines, the Constitution is not offended by letting the convictions stand.

I join the Court's opinion with regard to an "objective" or "reasonable person" test of "serious literary, artistic, political, or scientific value," Miller v. California, 413 U.S. 15, 24 (1973), because I think that the most faithful assessment of what Miller intended, and because we have not been asked to reconsider Miller in the present case. I must note, however, that in my view it is quite impossible to come to an objective assessment of (at least) literary or artistic value, there being many accomplished people who have found literature in Dada, and art in the replication of a soup can. Since ratiocination has little to do with esthetics, the fabled "reasonable man" is of little help in the inquiry, and would have to be replaced with, perhaps, the "man of tolerably good taste"—a description that betrays the lack of an ascertainable standard. If evenhanded and accurate decisionmaking is not always impossible under such a regime, it is at least impossible in the cases that matter. I think we would be better advised to adopt· as a legal maxim what has long been the wisdom of mankind: De gustibus non est disputandum. Just as there is no use arguing about taste, there is no use litigating about it. For the law courts to decide "What is Beauty" is a novelty even by today's standards.

The approach proposed by Part II of JUSTICE STEVENS' dissent does not eliminate this difficulty, but arguably aggravates it. It is a refined enough judgment to estimate whether a reasonable person would find literary or artistic value in a particular publication; it carries refinement to the point of meaninglessness to ask whether he could do so. Taste being, as I have said, unpredictable, the answer to the question must always be "yes"—so that there is little practical difference between that proposal and Part III of JUSTICE STEVENS' dissent, which asserts more forthrightly that "government may not constitutionally criminalize mere possession or sale of obscene literature, absent some connection to minors, or obtrusive display to unconsenting adults." Post, at 513 (footnote omitted).

All of today's opinions, I suggest, display the need for reexamination of Miller.

JUSTICE BLACKMUN, concurring in part and dissenting in part.

I join Part I of JUSTICE STEVENS' dissenting opinion for I agree with him that "harmless error" analysis may not appropriately be applied to this case. I join Parts I and II of JUSTICE WHITE's opinion for the Court (but not the Court's judgment remanding the case for harmless-error analysis), however, because I believe the standard enunciated in those Parts of that opinion meets the other concerns voiced by the dissent. JUSTICE WHITE points out: "Just as the ideas a work represents need not obtain majority approval to merit protection, neither, insofar as the First Amendment is concerned, does the value of the work vary from community to community based on the degree of local acceptance it has won." Ante, at 500. JUSTICE WHITE further emphasizes: "Of course . . . the mere fact that only a minority of a population may believe a work has serious value does not mean the 'reasonable person' standard would not be met." Ante, at 501, n. 3. Thus, contrary to the dissent's characterization, I do not think that "[a]juror asked to create a 'reasonable person' in order to apply the standard that the Court announces today might well believe that the majority of the population who find no value in such a book are more reasonable than the minority who do find value." Post, at 512. Rather, the Court's opinion stands for the clear proposition that the First Amendment does not permit a majority to dictate to discrete segments of the population—be they composed of art critics, literary scholars, or scientists—the value that may be found in various pieces of work. That only a minority may find value in a work does not mean that a jury would not conclude that "a reasonable person would find such value in the material, taken as a whole." Ante, at 501. Reasonable people certainly may differ as to what constitutes literary or artistic merit. See ante, at 504 (SCALIA, J., concurring). As I believe JUSTICE SCALIA recognizes in his concurrence (although he may not applaud it), the Court's opinion today envisions that even a minority view among reasonable people that a work has value may protect that work from being judged "obscene."

JUSTICE BRENNAN, dissenting.

JUSTICE STEVENS persuasively demonstrates the unconstitutionality of criminalizing the possession or sale of "obscene" materials to consenting adults. I write separately only to reiterate my view that any regulation of such material with respect to consenting adults suffers from the defect that "the concept of 'obscenity' cannot be defined with sufficient specificity and clarity to provide fair notice to persons who create and distribute sexually oriented materials, to prevent substantial erosion of protected speech as a byproduct of the attempt to suppress unprotected speech, and to avoid very costly institutional harms." Paris Adult Theatre I v. Slaton, 413 U.S. 49, 103 (1973) (BRENNAN, J., dissenting). I therefore join all but footnote 11 of JUSTICE STEVENS' dissent.

JUSTICE STEVENS, with whom JUSTICE MARSHALL joins, with whom JUSTICE BRENNAN joins except as to footnote 11, and with whom JUSTICE BLACKMUN joins as to Part I, dissenting.

The Court correctly holds that the juries that convicted petitioners were given erroneous instructions on one of the three essential elements of an obscenity conviction. Nevertheless, I disagree with its disposition of the case for three separate reasons: (1) the error in the instructions was not harmless; (2) the Court's attempt to clarify the constitutional definition of obscenity is not faithful to the First Amendment; and (3) I do not believe Illinois may criminalize the sale of magazines to consenting adults who enjoy the constitutional right to read and possess them.

I

The distribution of magazines is presumptively protected by the First Amendment. The Court has held, however, that the constitutional protection does not apply to obscene literature. If a state prosecutor can convince the trier of fact that the three components of the obscenity standard set forth in Miller v. California, 413 U.S. 15, 24 (1973), are satisfied, it may, in the Court's view, prohibit the sale of sexually explicit magazines. In a criminal prosecution, the prosecutor must prove each of these three elements beyond a reasonable doubt. Thus, in these cases, in addition to the first two elements of the Miller standard, the juries were required to find, on the basis of proof beyond a reasonable doubt, that each of the magazines "lacks serious literary, artistic, political, or scientific value." Ibid.

The required finding is fundamentally different from a conclusion that a majority of the populace considers the magazines offensive or worthless. As the Court correctly holds, the juries in these cases were not instructed to make the required finding; instead, they were asked to decide whether "ordinary adults in the whole State of Illinois" would view the magazines that petitioners sold as having value. App. 11, 25–26. Because of these erroneous instructions, the juries that found petitioners guilty of obscenity did not find one of the essential elements of that crime. This type of omission can never constitute harmless error.

Just as the constitutional right to trial by jury prohibits a judge from directing a verdict for the prosecution, United States v. Martin Linen Supply Co., 430 U.S. 564, 572–573 (1977), so too, "a jury's verdict cannot stand if the instructions provided the jury do not require it to find each element of the crime under the proper standard of proof." Cabana v. Bullock, 474 U.S. 376, 384 (1986). As JUSTICE WHITE has explained:

> "It should hardly need saying that a judgment or conviction cannot be entered against a defendant no matter how strong the evidence is against him, unless that evidence has been presented to a jury (or a judge, if a jury is waived) and unless the jury (or judge) finds from that evidence that the defendant's guilt has been proved beyond a reasonable doubt. It cannot be 'harmless error' wholly to deny a defendant a jury trial on one or all elements of the offense with which he is charged." Henderson v. Morgan, 426 U.S. 637, 650 (1976) (WHITE, J., concurring) (emphasis added).

Yet, this is exactly what happened in these cases. Because of the constitutionally erroneous instructions, petitioners were denied a jury determination on one of the critical elements of an obscenity prosecution.

An application of the harmless-error doctrine under these circumstances would not only violate petitioners' constitutional right to trial by jury, but would also pervert the notion of harmless error. When a court is asked to hold that an error that occurred did not interfere with the jury's ability to legitimately reach the verdict that it reached, harmless-error analysis may often be appropriate. But this principle cannot apply unless the jury found all of the elements required to support a conviction. The harmless-error doctrine may enable a court to remove a taint from proceedings in order to preserve a jury's findings, but it cannot constitutionally supplement those findings. It is fundamental that an appellate court (and for that matter, a trial court) is not free to decide in a criminal case that, if asked, a jury would have found something that it did not find. We have consistently rejected the possibility of harmless error in these circumstances. See Jackson v. Virginia, 443 U.S. 307, 320, n. 14 (1979); Carpenters v. United States, 330 U.S. 395, 408–409 (1947); Bollenbach v. United States, 326 U.S. 607, 615 (1946); see also Marks v. United States, 430 U.S. 188, 196, n. 12 (1977).

The Court suggests that these cases "are no longer good authority" in light of the decision last term in Rose v. Clark, 478 U.S. 570 (1986). See ante, at 503–504, n. 7. I emphatically disagree. In Rose v. Clark the Court held that harmless-error analysis is applicable to instructions that informed the jury of the proper elements of the crime and the proper standard of proof, but impermissibly gave the jury the option of finding one of the elements through a presumption, in violation of Sandstrom v. Montana, 442 U.S. 510 (1979), and Francis v. Franklin, 471 U.S. 307 (1985). In holding harmless-error analysis applicable, the Court explained that because the presumption in question "does not remove the issue of intent from the jury's consideration, it is distinguishable from other instructional errors that prevent a jury from considering an issue.'" 478 U.S., at 580, n. 8 (emphasis added), quoting Connecticut v. Johnson, 460 U.S. 73, 95, n. 3 (1983) (POWELL, J., dissenting). The Court reasoned that when the evidence is overwhelming on intent, the instruction allowing the jury to use a presumption can be deemed "simply superfluous," 478 U.S., at 581, for as JUSTICE POWELL had earlier stated, in some cases the evidence may be so "dispositive of intent that a reviewing court can say beyond a reasonable doubt that the jury would have found it unnecessary to rely on the presumption." Connecticut v. Johnson, 460 U.S., at 97, n. 5 (dissenting opinion). This case is, of course, far different. No court could ever determine that the instructions on the element were superfluous, since the error in the instructions went to the ultimate fact that the juries were required to find. Rose v. Clark did not modify the precedents requiring that a jury find all of the elements of a crime under the proper standard, any more than it modified the Sixth Amendment's provision that "[i]n all criminal prosecutions, the accused shall enjoy the right to a . . . trial by an impartial jury."

II

Aside from its error in remanding convictions which must clearly be reversed, the Court announces an obscenity standard that fails to accomplish the goal that the Court ascribes to it. After stressing the need to avoid a mere majoritarian inquiry, the Court states:

> "The proper inquiry is not whether an ordinary member of any given community would find serious literary, artistic, political, or scientific value in allegedly obscene material, but whether a reasonable person would find such value in the material, taken as a whole." Ante, at 500–501. The problem with this formulation is that it assumes that all reasonable persons would resolve the value inquiry in the same way. In fact, there are many cases in which some reasonable people would find that specific sexually oriented materials have serious artistic, political, literary, or scientific value, while other reasonable people would conclude that they have no such value. The Court's formulation does not tell the jury how to decide such cases.

In my judgment, communicative material of this sort is entitled to the protection of the First Amendment if some reasonable persons could consider it as having serious literary artistic, political, or scientific value. Over 40 years ago, the Court recognized that

> "Under our system of government there is an accommodation for the widest varieties of tastes and ideas. What is good literature, what has educational value, what is refined public information, what is good art, varies with individuals as it does from one generation to another. . . . From the multitude of competing offerings the public will pick and choose. What seems to one to be trash may have for others fleeting or even enduring values." Hannegan v. Esquire, Inc., 327 U.S. 146, 157–158 (1946). The purpose of the third element of the Miller test is to ensure that the obscenity laws not be allowed to "'level' the available reading matter to the majority or lowest common denominator of the population. . . . It is obvious that neither Ulysses nor Lady Chatterley's Lover would have literary appeal to the majority of the population." F. Schauer, The Law of Obscenity 144 (1976). A juror asked to create "a reasonable person" in order to apply the standard that the Court announces today might well believe that the majority of the population who find no value in such a book are more reasonable than the minority who do find value. First Amendment protection surely must not be contingent on this type of subjective determination.

III

There is an even more basic reason why I believe these convictions must be reversed. The difficulties inherent in the Court's "reasonable person" standard reaffirm my conviction that government may not constitutionally criminalize mere possession or sale of obscene literature, absent some connection to minors or obtrusive display to unconsenting adults. During the recent years in which the Court has struggled with the proper definition of obscenity, six Members of the Court have expressed the opinion that the First Amendment, at the very least, precludes criminal prosecutions for sales such as those involved in this case. Dissenting in Smith v. United States, 431 U.S. 291 (1977), I explained my view:

> "The question of offensiveness to community standards, whether national or local, is not one that the average juror can be expected to answer with even-handed consistency. The average juror may well have one reaction to sexually oriented materials in a completely private setting and an entirely different reaction in a social context. Studies have shown that an opinion held by a large majority of a group concerning a neutral and objective subject has a significant impact in distorting the perceptions of group members who would normally take a different position. Since obscenity is by no means a neutral subject, and since the ascertainment of a community standard is such a subjective task, the expression of individual jurors' sentiments will inevitably influence the perceptions of other jurors, particularly those who would normally be in the minority. Moreover, because the record never discloses the obscenity standards which the jurors actually apply, their decisions in these cases are effectively unreviewable by an appellate court. In the final analysis, the guilt or innocence of a criminal defendant in an obscenity trial is determined primarily by individual jurors' subjective reactions to the materials in question rather than by the predictable application of rules of law.

> "The conclusion is especially troubling because the same image—whether created by words, sounds, or pictures—may produce such a wide variety of reactions. As Mr. Justice Harlan noted: '[It is] often true that one man's vulgarity is another's lyric. Indeed, we think it is largely because government officials [or jurors] cannot make principled distinctions in this area that the Constitution leaves matters of taste and style so largely to the individual.' Cohen v. California, 403 U.S. 15, 25. In my judgment, the line between communications which 'offend' and those which do not is too blurred to identify criminal conduct. It is also too blurred to delimit the protections of the First Amendment." Id., at 315–316 (footnotes omitted).

The Court has repeatedly recognized that the Constitution "requires that a penal statute define the criminal offense with sufficient definiteness that ordinary people can understand what conduct is prohibited and in a manner that does not encourage arbitrary and discriminatory enforcement." Kolender v. Lawson, 461 U.S. 352, 357 (1983). These two requirements serve overlapping functions. Not only do vague statutes tend to give rise to selective and arbitrary prosecution, but selective and arbitrary prosecution often lessens the degree to which an actor is on notice that his or her conduct is illegal.

When petitioners Pope and Morrison accepted part-time employment as clerks in the bookstores, they could hardly have been expected to examine the stores' entire inventories, and even if they had, they would have had no way of knowing which, if any, of the magazines being sold were legally "obscene." Perhaps if the enterprise were being carried out in a clandestine manner, it might be fair to impute to them knowledge that something illegal was going on. But these stores both had large signs indicating the nature of the enterprise, one claiming that the store had "The Largest Selection of Adult Merchandise in Northern Illinois." See People's Exhibit No. 3, People v. Morrison, No. 84-cm-4114 (17th Jud. Cir. Ill. 1984). The Illinois Appellate Court found that Pope had the necessary scienter because it was "difficult to believe that [he] would not be fully apprised of the type and character of the three magazines simply by looking at them." App. to Pet. for Cert. 19. It is obvious that Pope knew that the magazines were "pornographic," but that does not mean he knew, or should have known, that they were legally "obscene" under the Illinois statute and our precedents. It would have been quite reasonable for him to conclude that if sale of the magazines were indeed against the law, then the police would never allow the store to remain in operation, much less publicly advertise its goods. Nor would an examination of the statute have given him much guidance.

Under ordinary circumstances, ignorance of the law is no excuse for committing a crime. But that principle presupposes a penal statute that adequately puts citizens on notice of what is illegal. The Constitution cannot tolerate schemes that criminalize categories of speech that the Court has conceded to be so vague and uncertain that they cannot "be defined legislatively." Smith v. United States, 431 U.S., at 303. If a legislature cannot define the crime, Richard Pope and Michael Morrison should not be expected to. Criminal prosecution under these circumstances "may be as much of a trap for the innocent as the ancient laws of Caligula." United States v. Cardiff, 344 U.S. 174, 176 (1952).

Concern with the vagueness inherent in criminal obscenity statutes is not the only constitutional objection to the criminalization of the sale of sexually explicit material (not involving children) to consenting adults. In Stanley v. Georgia, 394 U.S. 557 (1969), the Court held that Georgia could not criminalize the mere possession of obscene matter. The decision was grounded upon a recognition that "[o]ur whole constitutional heritage rebels at the thought of giving government the power to control men's minds." Id., at 565. The only justification we could find for the law there was Georgia's desire to "protect the individual's mind from the effects of obscenity," ibid., and we concluded that such a desire to "control the moral content of a person's thoughts . . . is wholly inconsistent with the philosophy of the First Amendment." Id., at 565–566.

The Court has adopted a restrictive reading of Stanley, opining that it has no implications to the criminalization of the sale or distribution of obscenity. See United States v. Reidel, 402 U.S. 351 (1971); United States v. 12 200-Ft. Reels of Film, 413 U.S. 123 (1973). But such a crabbed approach offends the overarching First Amendment principles discussed in Stanley, almost as much as it insults the citizenry by declaring its right to read and possess material which it may not legally obtain. In Stanley, the Court recognized that there are legitimate reasons for the State to regulate obscenity: protecting children and protecting the sensibilities of unwilling viewers. 394 U.S., at 507. But surely a broad criminal prohibition on all sale of obscene material cannot survive simply because the State may constitutionally restrict public display or prohibit sale of the material to minors.

As was the case in Smith, "I do not know whether the ugly pictures in this record have any beneficial value." 431 U.S., at 319 (STEVENS, J., dissenting). I do know though:

> "The fact that there is a large demand for comparable materials indicates that they do provide amusement or information, or at least satisfy the curiosity of interested persons. Moreover, there are serious well-intentioned people who are persuaded that they serve a worthwhile purpose. Others believe they arouse passions that lead to the commission of crimes; if that be true, surely there is a mountain of material just within the protected zone that is equally capable of motivating comparable conduct. Moreover, the baneful effects of these materials are disturbingly reminiscent of arguments formerly made about what are now valued as works of art. In the end, I believe we must rely on the capacity of the free marketplace of ideas to distinguish that which is useful or beautiful from that which is ugly or worthless." Id., at 320–321 (footnotes omitted).

I respectfully dissent.

APPENDIX 3:
CHILDREN'S INTERNET PROTECTION ACT—SELECTED PROVISIONS [PUB. L. NO. 106-554, 12/21/2000]

TITLE 42—CHILDREN'S INTERNET PROTECTION

SEC. 1701. SHORT TITLE

This title may be cited as the "Children's Internet Protection Act".

***

SEC. 1711. LIMITATION ON AVAILABILITY OF CERTAIN FUNDS FOR SCHOOLS.

Title III of the Elementary and Secondary Education Act of 1965 (20 U.S.C. 6801 et seq.) is amended by adding at the end the following:

"PART F—LIMITATION ON AVAILABILITY OF CERTAIN FUNDS FOR SCHOOLS

"SEC. 3601. LIMITATION ON AVAILABILITY OF CERTAIN FUNDS FOR SCHOOLS.

"(a) INTERNET SAFETY.—

"(1) IN GENERAL.—No funds made available under this title to a local educational agency for an elementary or secondary school that does not receive services at discount rates under section 254(h)(5) of the Communications Act of 1934, as added by section 1721 of Children's Internet Protection Act, may be used to purchase computers used to access the Internet, or to pay for direct costs associated with accessing the Internet, for such school unless the school, school board, local educational agency, or other authority with responsibility for administration of such school both—

"(A)(i) has in place a policy of Internet safety for minors that includes the operation of a technology protection measure with respect to any of its computers with Internet access that protects against access through such computers to visual depictions that are—

"(I) obscene;

"(II) child pornography; or

"(III) harmful to minors; and

"(ii) is enforcing the operation of such technology protection measure during any use of such computers by minors; and

"(B)(i) has in place a policy of Internet safety that includes the operation of a technology protection measure with respect to any of its computers with Internet access that protects against access through such computers to visual depictions that are—

"(I) obscene; or

"(II) child pornography; and

"(ii) is enforcing the operation of such technology protection measure during any use of such computers.

"(3) **DISABLING DURING CERTAIN USE.**—An administrator, supervisor, or person authorized by the responsible authority under paragraph (1) may disable the technology protection measure concerned to enable access for bona fide research or other lawful purposes."

SEC. 1712. LIMITATION ON AVAILABILITY OF CERTAIN FUNDS FOR LIBRARIES.

"(f) INTERNET SAFETY.—

"(1) **IN GENERAL.**—No funds made available under this Act for a library described in section 213(2)(A) or (B) that does not receive services at discount rates under section 254(h)(6) of the Communications Act of 1934, as added by section 1721 of this Children's Internet Protection Act, may be used to purchase computers used to access the Internet, or to pay for direct costs associated with accessing the Internet, for such library unless—

"(A) such library—

"(i) has in place a policy of Internet safety for minors that includes the operation of a technology protection measure with respect to any of its computers with Internet access that protects against access through such computers to visual depictions that are—

"(I) obscene;

"(II) child pornography; or

"(III) harmful to minors; and

"(ii) is enforcing the operation of such technology protection measure during any use of such computers by minors; and

"(B) such library—

"(i) has in place a policy of Internet safety that includes the operation of a technology protection measure with respect to any of its computers with Internet access that protects against access through such computers to visual depictions that are—

"(I) obscene; or

"(II) child pornography; and

"(ii) is enforcing the operation of such technology protection measure during any use of such computers.

"(3) **DISABLING DURING CERTAIN USE.**—An administrator, supervisor, or other authority may disable a technology protection measure under paragraph (1) to enable access for bona fide research or other lawful purposes."

***

SEC. 1721 REQUIREMENT FOR SCHOOLS AND LIBRARIES TO ENFORCE INTERNET SAFETY POLICIES WITH TECHNOLOGY PROTECTION MEASURES FOR COMPUTERS WITH INTERNET ACCESS AS CONDITION OF UNIVERSAL SERVICE DISCOUNTS.

"(5) REQUIREMENTS FOR CERTAIN SCHOOLS WITH COMPUTERS HAVING INTERNET ACCESS.—

"(A) INTERNET SAFETY.—

"(i) IN GENERAL.—Except as provided in clause (ii), an elementary or secondary school having computers with Internet access may not receive services at discount rates under paragraph (1)(B) unless the school, school board, local educational agency, or other authority with responsibility for administration of the school—

"(I) submits to the Commission the certifications described in subparagraphs (B) and (C);

"(II) submits to the Commission a certification that an Internet safety policy has been adopted and implemented for the school under subsection (l); and

"(III) ensures the use of such computers in accordance with the certifications.

"(B) CERTIFICATION WITH RESPECT TO MINORS.—A certification under this subparagraph is a certification that the school, school board, local educational agency, or other authority with responsibility for administration of the school—

"(i) is enforcing a policy of Internet safety for minors that includes monitoring the online activities of minors and the operation of a technology protection measure with respect to any of its computers with Internet access that protects against access through such computers to visual depictions that are—

"(I) obscene;

"(II) child pornography; or

"(III) harmful to minors; and

"(ii) is enforcing the operation of such technology protection measure during any use of such computers by minors.

"(C) **CERTIFICATION WITH RESPECT TO ADULTS.**—A certification under this paragraph is a certification that the school, school board, local educational agency, or other authority with responsibility for administration of the school—

"(i) is enforcing a policy of Internet safety that includes the operation of a technology protection measure with respect to any of its computers with Internet access that protects against access through such computers to visual depictions that are—

"(I) obscene; or

"(II) child pornography; and

"(ii) is enforcing the operation of such technology protection measure during any use of such computers.

"(D) **DISABLING DURING ADULT USE.**—An administrator, supervisor, or other person authorized by the certifying authority under subparagraph (A)(i) may disable the technology protection measure concerned, during use by an adult, to enable access for bona fide research or other lawful purpose.

"(6) **REQUIREMENTS FOR CERTAIN LIBRARIES WITH COMPUTERS HAVING INTERNET ACCESS.**—

'(A) **INTERNET SAFETY.**—

"(i) **IN GENERAL.**—Except as provided in clause (ii), a library having one or more computers with Internet access may not receive services at discount rates under paragraph (1)(B) unless the library—

"(I) submits to the Commission the certifications described in subparagraphs (B) and (C); and

"(II) submits to the Commission a certification that an Internet safety policy has been adopted and implemented for the library under subsection (l); and

"(III) ensures the use of such computers in accordance with the certifications.

"(B) **CERTIFICATION WITH RESPECT TO MINORS.**—A certification under this subparagraph is a certification that the library—

"(i) is enforcing a policy of Internet safety that includes the operation of a technology protection measure with respect to any of its computers with Internet access that protects against access through such computers to visual depictions that are—

"(I) obscene;

"(II) child pornography; or

"(III) harmful to minors; and

"(ii) is enforcing the operation of such technology protection measure during any use of such computers by minors.

"(C) **CERTIFICATION WITH RESPECT TO ADULTS.**—A certification under this paragraph is a certification that the library—

"(i) is enforcing a policy of Internet safety that includes the operation of a technology protection measure with respect to any of its computers with Internet access that protects against access through such computers to visual depictions that are—

"(I) obscene; or

"(II) child pornography; and

"(ii) is enforcing the operation of such technology protection measure during any use of such computers.

"(D) **DISABLING DURING ADULT USE.**—An administrator, supervisor, or other person authorized by the certifying authority under subparagraph (A)(i) may disable the technology protection measure concerned, during use by an adult, to enable access for bona fide research or other lawful purpose."

***

SEC. 1731. SHORT TITLE.

This subtitle may be cited as the "Neighborhood Children's Internet Protection Act'.'

SEC. 1732. INTERNET SAFETY POLICY REQUIRED.

Section 254 of the Communications Act of 1934 (47 U.S.C. 254) is amended by adding at the end the following:

"(l) **INTERNET SAFETY POLICY REQUIREMENT FOR SCHOOLS AND LIBRARIES.**—

"(1) **IN GENERAL.**—In carrying out its responsibilities under subsection (h), each school or library to which subsection (h) applies shall—

"(A) adopt and implement an Internet safety policy that addresses—

"(i) access by minors to inappropriate matter on the Internet and World Wide Web;

"(ii) the safety and security of minors when using electronic mail, chat rooms, and other forms of direct electronic communications;

"(iii) unauthorized access, including so-called 'hacking,' and other unlawful activities by minors online;

"(iv) unauthorized disclosure, use, and dissemination of personal identification information regarding minors; and

"(v) measures designed to restrict minors' access to materials harmful to minors; and

"(B) provide reasonable public notice and hold at least one public hearing or meeting to address the proposed Internet safety policy.

"(2) LOCAL DETERMINATION OF CONTENT.—A determination regarding what matter is inappropriate for minors shall be made by the school board, local educational agency, library, or other authority responsible for making the determination."

***

SEC. 1741. EXPEDITED REVIEW.

(a) THREE-JUDGE DISTRICT COURT HEARING.—Notwithstanding any other provision of law, any civil action challenging the constitutionality, on its face, of this title or any amendment made by this title, or any provision thereof, shall be heard by a district court of 3 judges convened pursuant to the provisions of section 2284 of title 28, United States Code.

(b) APPELLATE REVIEW.—Notwithstanding any other provision of law, an interlocutory or final judgment, decree, or order of the court of 3 judges in an action under subsection (a) holding this title or an amendment made by this title, or any provision thereof, unconstitutional shall be reviewable as a matter of right by direct appeal to the Supreme Court. Any such appeal shall be filed not more than 20 days after entry of such judgment, decree, or order.

APPENDIX 4:
THE CAN-SPAM ACT OF 2003—SELECTED PROVISIONS
[PUB. L. NO. 108-187, 12/16/2003]

PUBLIC LAW 108-187 OF 2003, 108TH CONGRESS

SECTION 1. SHORT TITLE.

This Act may be cited as the 'Controlling the Assault of Non-Solicited Pornography and Marketing Act of 2003,' or the 'CAN-SPAM Act of 2003.'

***

SEC. 4. PROHIBITION AGAINST PREDATORY AND ABUSIVE COMMERCIAL E-MAIL.

(a) OFFENSE—

(1) IN GENERAL—Chapter 47 of title 18, United States Code, is amended by adding at the end the following new section:

'Sec. 1037. Fraud and related activity in connection with electronic mail

'(a) IN GENERAL—Whoever, in or affecting interstate or foreign commerce, knowingly—

'(1) accesses a protected computer without authorization, and intentionally initiates the transmission of multiple commercial electronic mail messages from or through such computer,

'(2) uses a protected computer to relay or retransmit multiple commercial electronic mail messages, with the intent to deceive or mislead recipients, or any Internet access service, as to the origin of such messages,

'(3) materially falsifies header information in multiple commercial electronic mail messages and intentionally initiates the transmission of such messages,

'(4) registers, using information that materially falsifies the identity of the actual registrant, for five or more electronic mai accounts or online user accounts or two or more domain names, and intentionally initiates the transmission of multiple commercial electronic mail messages from any combination of such accounts or domain names, or

'(5) falsely represents oneself to be the registrant or the legitimate successor in interest to the registrant of 5 or more Internet Protocol addresses, and intentionally initiates the transmission of multiple commercial electronic mail messages from such addresses, or conspires to do so, shall be punished as provided in subsection (b).

'(b) PENALTIES—The punishment for an offense under subsection (a) is—

'(1) a fine under this title, imprisonment for not more than 5 years, or both, if—

'(A) the offense is committed in furtherance of any felony under the laws of the United States or of any State; or

'(B) the defendant has previously been convicted under this section or section 1030, or under the law of any State for conduct involving the transmission of multiple commercial electronic mail messages or unauthorized access to a computer system;

'(2) a fine under this title, imprisonment for not more than 3 years, or both, if—

'(A) the offense is an offense under subsection (a)(1);

'(B) the offense is an offense under subsection (a)(4) and involved 20 or more falsified electronic mail or online user account registrations, or 10 or more falsified domain name registrations;

'(C) the volume of electronic mail messages transmitted in furtherance of the offense exceeded 2,500 during any 24-hour period, 25,000 during any 30-day period, or 250,000 during any 1-year period;

'(D) the offense caused loss to one or more persons aggregating $5,000 or more in value during any 1-year period;

'(E) as a result of the offense any individual committing the offense obtained anything of value aggregating $5,000 or more during any 1-year period; or

'(F) the offense was undertaken by the defendant in concert with three or more other persons with respect to whom the defendant occupied a position of organizer or leader; and

'(3) a fine under this title or imprisonment for not more than 1 year, or both, in any other case.

'(c) FORFEITURE—

'(1) IN GENERAL—The court, in imposing sentence on a person who is convicted of an offense under this section, shall order that the defendant forfeit to the United States—

'(A) any property, real or personal, constituting or traceable to gross proceeds obtained from such offense; and

'(B) any equipment, software, or other technology used or intended to be used to commit or to facilitate the commission of such offense.

'(2) PROCEDURES—The procedures set forth in section 413 of the Controlled Substances Act (21 U.S.C. § 853), other than subsection (d) of that section, and in Rule 32.2 of the Federal Rules of Criminal Procedure, shall apply to all stages of a criminal forfeiture proceeding under this section.

'(d) DEFINITIONS—In this section:

'(1) LOSS—The term 'loss' has the meaning given that term in section 1030(e) of this title.

'(2) MATERIALLY—For purposes of paragraphs (3) and (4) of subsection (a), header information or registration information is materially falsified if it is altered or concealed in a manner that would impair the ability of a recipient of the message, an Internet access service processing the message on behalf of a recipient, a person alleging a violation of this section, or a law enforcement agency to identify, locate, or respond to a person who initiated the electronic mail message or to investigate the alleged violation.

'(3) MULTIPLE—The term 'multiple' means more than 100 electronic mail messages during a 24-hour period, more than 1,000 electronic mail messages during a 30-day period, or more than 10,000 electronic mail messages during a 1-year period.

'(4) OTHER TERMS—Any other term has the meaning given that term by section 3 of the CAN-SPAM Act of 2003.'.

(2) CONFORMING AMENDMENT—The chapter analysis for chapter 47 of title 18, United States Code, is amended by adding at the end the following:

'Sec. 1037. Fraud and related activity in connection with electronic mail.'.

(b) UNITED STATES SENTENCING COMMISSION—

(1) DIRECTIVE—Pursuant to its authority under section 994(p) of title 28, United States Code, and in accordance with this section, the United States Sentencing Commission shall review and, as appropriate, amend the sentencing guidelines and policy statements to provide appropriate penalties for violations of section 1037 of title 18,

United States Code, as added by this section, and other offenses that may be facilitated by the sending of large quantities of unsolicited electronic mail.

(2) REQUIREMENTS—In carrying out this subsection, the Sentencing Commission shall consider providing sentencing enhancements for—

(A) those convicted under section 1037 of title 18, United States Code, who—

(i) obtained electronic mail addresses through improper means, including—

(I) harvesting electronic mail addresses of the users of a website, proprietary service, or other online public forum operated by another person, without the authorization of such person; and

(II) randomly generating electronic mail addresses by computer; or

(ii) knew that the commercial electronic mail messages involved in the offense contained or advertised an Internet domain for which the registrant of the domain had provided false registration information; and

(B) those convicted of other offenses, including offenses involving fraud, identity theft, obscenity, child pornography, and the sexual exploitation of children, if such offenses involved the sending of large quantities of electronic mail.

(c) SENSE OF CONGRESS—It is the sense of Congress that—

(1) Spam has become the method of choice for those who distribute pornography, perpetrate fraudulent schemes, and introduce viruses, worms, and Trojan horses into personal and business computer systems; and

(2) the Department of Justice should use all existing law enforcement tools to investigate and prosecute those who send bulk commercial e-mail to facilitate the commission of Federal crimes, including the tools contained in chapters 47 and 63 of title 18, United States Code (relating to fraud and false statements); chapter 71 of title 18, United States Code (relating to obscenity); chapter 110 of title 18, United States Code (relating to the sexual exploitation of children); and chapter 95 of title 18, United States Code (relating to racketeering), as appropriate.

SEC. 5. OTHER PROTECTIONS FOR USERS OF COMMERCIAL ELECTRONIC MAIL.

(a) REQUIREMENTS FOR TRANSMISSION OF MESSAGES—

(1) PROHIBITION OF FALSE OR MISLEADING TRANSMISSION INFORMATION—It is unlawful for any person to initiate the transmission, to a protected computer, of a commercial electronic mail message, or a transactional or relationship message, that contains, or is accompanied by, header information that is materially false or materially misleading. For purposes of this paragraph—

(A) header information that is technically accurate but includes an originating electronic mail address, domain name, or Internet Protocol address the access to which for purposes of initiating the message was obtained by means of false or fraudulent pretenses or representations shall be considered materially misleading;

(B) a 'from' line (the line identifying or purporting to identify a person initiating the message) that accurately identifies any person who initiated the message shall not be considered materially false or materially misleading; and

(C) header information shall be considered materially misleading if it fails to identify accurately a protected computer used to initiate the message because the person initiating the message knowingly uses another protected computer to relay or retransmit the message for purposes of disguising its origin.

(2) PROHIBITION OF DECEPTIVE SUBJECT HEADINGS—It is unlawful for any person to initiate the transmission to a protected computer of a commercial electronic mail message if such person has actual knowledge, or knowledge fairly implied on the basis of objective circumstances, that a subject heading of the message would be likely to mislead a recipient, acting reasonably under the circumstances, about a material fact regarding the contents or subject matter of the message (consistent with the criteria used in enforcement of section 5 of the Federal Trade Commission Act (15 U.S.C. § 45)).

(3) INCLUSION OF RETURN ADDRESS OR COMPARABLRE MECHANISM IN COMMERCIAL ELECTRONIC MAIL—

(A) IN GENERAL—It is unlawful for any person to initiate the transmission to a protected computer of a commercial electronic mail message that does not contain a functioning return electronic mail address or other Internet-based mechanism, clearly and conspicuously displayed, that—

(i) a recipient may use to submit, in a manner specified in the message, a reply electronic mail message or other form of Internet-based communication requesting not to receive future commercial electronic mail messages from that sender at the electronic mail address where the message was received; and

(ii) remains capable of receiving such messages or communications for no less than 30 days after the transmission of the original message.

(B) MORE DETAILED OPTIONS POSSIBLE—The person initiating a commercial electronic mail message may comply with subparagraph (A)(i) by providing the recipient a list or menu from which the recipient may choose the specific types of commercial electronic mail messages the recipient wants to receive or does not want to receive from the sender, if the list or menu includes an option under which the recipient may choose not to receive any commercial electronic mail messages from the sender.

(C) TEMPORARY INABILITY TO RECEIVE MESSAGES OR PROCESS REQUESTS—A return electronic mail address or other mechanism does not fail to satisfy the requirements of subparagraph (A) if it is unexpectedly and temporarily unable to receive messages or process requests due to a technical problem beyond the control of the sender if the problem is corrected within a reasonable time period.

(4) PROHIBITION OF TRANSMISSION OF COMMERCIAL ELECTRONIC MAIL AFTER OBJECTION—

(A) IN GENERAL—If a recipient makes a request using a mechanism provided pursuant to paragraph (3) not to receive some or any commercial electronic mail messages from such sender, then it is unlawful—

(i) for the sender to initiate the transmission to the recipient, more than 10 business days after the receipt of such request, of a commercial electronic mail message that falls within the scope of the request;

(ii) for any person acting on behalf of the sender to initiate the transmission to the recipient, more than 10 business days after the receipt of such request, of a commercial electronic mail message with actual knowledge, or knowledge fairly implied on the basis of objective circumstances, that such message falls within the scope of the request;

(iii) for any person acting on behalf of the sender to assist in initiating the transmission to the recipient, through the provision or selection of addresses to which the message will be sent, of a commercial electronic mail message with actual knowledge, or knowledge fairly implied on the basis of objective circumstances, that such message would violate clause (i) or (ii); or

(iv) for the sender, or any other person who knows that the recipient has made such a request, to sell, lease, exchange, or otherwise transfer or release the electronic mail address of the recipient (including through any transaction or other transfer involving mailing lists bearing the electronic mail address of the recipient) for any purpose other than compliance with this Act or other provision of law.

(B) SUBSEQUENT AFFIRMATIVE CONSENT—A prohibition in subparagraph (A) does not apply if there is affirmative consent by the recipient subsequent to the request under subparagraph (A).

(5) INCLUSION OF IDENTIFIER, OPT-OUT, AND PHYSICAL ADDRESS IN COMMERCIAL ELECTRONIC MAIL—

(A) It is unlawful for any person to initiate the transmission of any commercial electronic mail message to a protected computer unless the message provides—

(i) clear and conspicuous identification that the message is an advertisement or solicitation;

(ii) clear and conspicuous notice of the opportunity under paragraph (3) to decline to receive further commercial electronic mail messages from the sender; and

(iii) a valid physical postal address of the sender.

(B) Subparagraph (A)(i) does not apply to the transmission of a commercial electronic mail message if the recipient has given prior affirmative consent to receipt of the message.

(6) MATERIALLY—For purposes of paragraph (1), the term 'materially,' when used with respect to false or misleading header information, includes the alteration or concealment of header information in a manner that would impair the ability of an Internet access service processing the message on behalf of a recipient, a person alleging a

violation of this section, or a law enforcement agency to identify, locate, or respond to a person who initiated the electronic mail message or to investigate the alleged violation, or the ability of a recipient of the message to respond to a person who initiated the electronic message.

(b) AGGRAVATED VIOLATIONS RELATING TO COMMERCIAL ELECTRONIC MAIL—

(1) ADDRESS HARVESTING AND DICTIONARY ATTACKS—

(A) IN GENERAL—It is unlawful for any person to initiate the transmission, to a protected computer, of a commercial electronic mail message that is unlawful under subsection (a), or to assist in the origination of such message through the provision or selection of addresses to which the message will be transmitted, if such person had actual knowledge, or knowledge fairly implied on the basis of objective circumstances, that—

(i) the electronic mail address of the recipient was obtained using an automated means from an Internet website or proprietary online service operated by another person, and such website or online service included, at the time the address was obtained, a notice stating that the operator of such website or online service will not give, sell, or otherwise transfer addresses maintained by such website or online service to any other party for the purposes of initiating, or enabling others to initiate, electronic mail messages; or

(ii) the electronic mail address of the recipient was obtained using an automated means that generates possible electronic mail addresses by combining names, letters, or numbers into numerous permutations.

(B) DISCLAIMER—Nothing in this paragraph creates an ownership or proprietary interest in such electronic mail addresses.

(2) AUTOMATED CREATION OF MULTIPLE ELECTRONIC MAIL ACCOUNTS—It is unlawful for any person to use scripts or other automated means to register for multiple electronic mail accounts or online user accounts from which to transmit to a protected computer, or enable another person to transmit to a protected computer, a commercial electronic mail message that is unlawful under subsection (a).

(3) RELAY OR RETRANSMISSION THROUGH UNAUTHORIZED ACCESS—It is unlawful for any person knowingly to relay or retransmit a commercial electronic mail message that is unlawful under

subsection (a) from a protected computer or computer network that such person has accessed without authorization.

(c) SUPPLEMENTARY RULEMAKING AUTHORITY—The Commission shall by regulation, pursuant to section 13—

(1) modify the 10-business-day period under subsection (a)(4)(A) or subsection (a)(4)(B), or both, if the Commission determines that a different period would be more reasonable after taking into account—

(A) the purposes of subsection (a);

(B) the interests of recipients of commercial electronic mail; and

(C) the burdens imposed on senders of lawful commercial electronic mail; and

(2) specify additional activities or practices to which subsection (b) applies if the Commission determines that those activities or practices are contributing substantially to the proliferation of commercial electronic mail messages that are unlawful under subsection (a).

(d) REQUIREMENT TO PLACE WARNING LABELS ON COMMERCIAL ELECTRONIC MAIL CONTAINING SEXUALLY ORIENTED MATERIAL—

(1) IN GENERAL—No person may initiate in or affecting interstate commerce the transmission, to a protected computer, of any commercial electronic mail message that includes sexually oriented material and—

(A) fail to include in subject heading for the electronic mail message the marks or notices prescribed by the Commission under this subsection; or

(B) fail to provide that the matter in the message that is initially viewable to the recipient, when the message is opened by any recipient and absent any further actions by the recipient, includes only—

(i) to the extent required or authorized pursuant to paragraph (2), any such marks or notices;

(ii) the information required to be included in the message pursuant to subsection (a)(5); and

(iii) instructions on how to access, or a mechanism to access, the sexually oriented material.

(2) PRIOR AFFIRMATIVE CONSENT—Paragraph (1) does not apply to the transmission of an electronic mail message if the recipient has given prior affirmative consent to receipt of the message.

(3) PRESCRIPTION OF MARKS AND NOTICES—Not later than 120 days after the date of the enactment of this Act, the Commission in consultation with the Attorney General shall prescribe clearly identifiable marks or notices to be included in or associated with commercial electronic mail that contains sexually oriented material, in order to inform the recipient of that fact and to facilitate filtering of such electronic mail. The Commission shall publish in the Federal Register and provide notice to the public of the marks or notices prescribed under this paragraph.

(4) DEFINITION—In this subsection, the term 'sexually oriented material' means any material that depicts sexually explicit conduct (as that term is defined in section 2256 of title 18, United States Code), unless the depiction constitutes a small and insignificant part of the whole, the remainder of which is not primarily devoted to sexual matters.

(5) PENALTY—Whoever knowingly violates paragraph (1) shall be fined under title 18, United States Code, or imprisoned not more than 5 years, or both.

***

SEC. 8. EFFECT ON OTHER LAWS.

(a) FEDERAL LAW—

(1) Nothing in this Act shall be construed to impair the enforcement of section 223 or 231 of the Communications Act of 1934 (47 U.S.C. § 223 or 231, respectively), chapter 71 (relating to obscenity) or 110 (relating to sexual exploitation of children) of title 18, United States Code, or any other Federal criminal statute.

(2) Nothing in this Act shall be construed to affect in any way the Commission's authority to bring enforcement actions under FTC Act for materially false or deceptive representations or unfair practices in commercial electronic mail messages.

(b) STATE LAW—

(1) IN GENERAL—This Act supersedes any statute, regulation, or rule of a State or political subdivision of a State that expressly regulates the use of electronic mail to send commercial messages, except

to the extent that any such statute, regulation, or rule prohibits falsity or deception in any portion of a commercial electronic mail message or information attached thereto.

(2) STATE LAW NOT SPECIFIC TO ELECTRONIC MAIL—This Act shall not be construed to preempt the applicability of—

(A) State laws that are not specific to electronic mail, including State trespass, contract, or tort law; or

(B) other State laws to the extent that those laws relate to acts of fraud or computer crime.

(c) NO EFFECT ON POLICIES OF PROVIDERS OF INTERNET ACCESS SERVICE—Nothing in this Act shall be construed to have any effect on the lawfulness or unlawfulness, under any other provision of law, of the adoption, implementation, or enforcement by a provider of Internet access service of a policy of declining to transmit, route, relay, handle, or store certain types of electronic mail messages.

SEC. 9. DO-NOT-E-MAIL REGISTRY.

(a) IN GENERAL—Not later than 6 months after the date of enactment of this Act, the Commission shall transmit to the Senate Committee on Commerce, Science, and Transportation and the House of Representatives Committee on Energy and Commerce a report that—

(1) sets forth a plan and t imetable for establishing a nationwide marketing Do-Not-E-Mail registry;

(2) includes an explanation of any practical, technical, security, privacy, enforceability, or other concerns that the Commission has regarding such a registry; and

(3) includes an explanation of how the registry would be applied with respect to children with e-mail accounts.

APPENDIX 5:
STATE OBSCENITY STATUTES

STATE	STATUTE
Alabama	Ala. Code §§ 13A-12-200.1 et seq.
Alaska	None
Arizona	Ariz. Rev. Stat. §§ 13-3501 et seq.
Arkansas	Ark. Code Ann. §§ 5-68-201 et seq.
California	Cal. Penal Code §§ 311 et seq.
Colorado	Colo. Rev. Stat. § 18-7-101
Connecticut	Conn. Gen. Stat. Ann. §§ 53a-952-193 et seq.
Delaware	Del Code Ann. Tit. 11, Ch. 5, §§ 1361 et seq.
Florida	Fla. Stat. Ann. ch. § 847
Georgia	Ga. Code Ann. §§16-12-80; 16-12-100
Hawaii	None
Idaho	Idaho Code §§ 18-4101 et seq.
Illinois	720 ILCS 5/11-20
Indiana	Ind. Code §§ 35-49-1 et seq.; 35-49-2 et seq.; 35-49-3 et seq.
Iowa	Iowa Code §§ 728.1 et seq.
Kansas	Kan. Stat. Ann. § 21-4301

STATE	STATUTE
Kentucky	Kentucky Rev. Stat. §§ 531.010 et seq.
Louisiana	La. Rev. Stat. §§ 14:91.11; 14:106; 32:378.1
Maine	Me. Rev. Stat., Title 17, Chapter 93-A, §§ 2911 et seq.
Maryland	Md. Code Ann. §§ 11-101; 11-201 et seq.
Massachusetts	Mass. Gen. Laws ch. 272, §§ 28 et seq.
Michigan	Mich. Stat. Ann. §§ 752.361 et seq.
Minnesota	Minn. Stat. Ann. §§ 617.241; 617.243; 617.245; 617.25; 617.251; 617.26-29; 617.291; 617.292
Mississippi	Miss. Code Ann. §§ Title 97-19-101; 97-19-103; 97-19-105; 97-19-107;
Missouri	Mo. Rev. Stat.§§ 573.010 et seq.
Montana	None
Nebraska	Neb. Rev. Stat. § 28-808
Nevada	Nev. Rev. Stat. §§ 201.235 et seq.
New Hampshire	N.H. Rev. Stat. Ann. §§ 650:1 et seq.
New Jersey	N.J. Stat. §§ 2C:34-2 et seq.
New Mexico	None
New York	N.Y. Penal Law §§ 235.00 et seq.
North Carolina	N.C. Gen. Stat. §§ 14-190.1 et seq.
North Dakota	N.D. Cent. Code § 12.1-27.1
Ohio	Ohio Rev. Code Ann. §§ 2907.01 et seq.
Oklahoma	21 Okla. Stat. §§ 1024.1 et seq.; 1040.8 et seq.; 1040.54
Oregon	None
Pennsylvania	18 Pa.C.S. § 5903
Rhode Island	R.I. Gen. Laws § 11-31-1
South Carolina	S.C. Code Ann. §§ 16-15-305 et seq.

STATE	STATUTE
South Dakota	S.D. Codified Laws § 22-24-25
Tennessee	Tenn. Code Ann. §§ 39-17-901 et seq.
Texas	Tex. Penal Code §§ 43.21 et seq.
Utah	Utah Code Ann. §§ 76-10-1201; 76-10-1203 et seq.; 76-10-1210; 76-10-1212 et seq.; 76-10-1222; 76-10-1225; 76-10-1229
Vermont	None
Virginia	Va. Code Ann. §§ 18–8-2–372 et seq.
Washington	Wash. Rev. Code Ann. §§ 9.68.050; 9.68.060; 9.68.130; 9.68.140; 7.42.010; 7.42.060; 7.48A.101; 10.37.130
West Virginia	None
Wisconsin	Wis. Stat. Ann. §§ 944.20 et seq.; 944.25
Wyoming	Wyo. Stat. Ann. §§ 6-4-301 et seq.

Sources: National Obscenity Law Center and State Statutes.

APPENDIX 6:
STATE OBSCENITY REPORT FORM

STATE OBSCENITY REPORT FORM

To State Prosecutor: From organizations or citizen(s) making report:

_____   _____

_____   _____

_____   _____

I (We) wish to report a possible violation of State obscenity laws. I (We) ask that you investigate and, if you find probable cause, that you take steps to initiate criminal obscenity or other appropriate legal proceedings against the individuals or businesses responsible.

In my opinion, the material described below may be obscene under the U.S. Supreme Court's three-part obscenity test and in violation of State obscenity laws, in that a judge and jury may find the material:
1. When taken as a whole, appeals to the prurient interest in sex; and
2. Depicts or describes hardcore sexual conduct in a patently offensive manner; and
3. When taken as a whole, lacks serious literary and artistic and political and scientific value.

We Are Reporting About:

☐ Video or DVD   ☐ Magazine   ☐ Live Performance
☐ Motion Picture   ☐ Vending Machine Publication   ☐ Sound Recording
☐ Cable/Satellite TV Channel ☐ Advertisement   ☐ Dildo or Artificial Vagina
☐ Photograph   ☐ Comic Book   ☐ Other _____
☐ Computer-Generated Image   ☐ Paperback Book   _____

Entitled: _____

Name/Address of company providing the material, and date observed: _____

_____

Which Depicted or Described Sexual Conduct:

☐ Sexual Intercourse   ☐ Sadomasochism   ☐ Masturbation
☐ Anal Sex   ☐ Sexual Bestiality   ☐ Excretory Functions
☐ Oral Sex   ☐ Lewd Exhibition of the Genitals
☐ Other_____

Please acknowledge receipt of this complaint.

By: _____

Date: _____   _____
                                              (TITLE)

APPENDIX 7:
FEDERAL OBSCENITY REPORT FORM

FEDERAL OBSCENITY REPORT FORM

To: U. S. Attorney_____   From:_____
    (*name, if known*)

_____   _____

_____   (Telephone)_____

Federal obscenity laws apply in every state and make it a crime to (among other things):

♦ *Mail* or *import* obscene matter (18 USC 1461)

♦ Use a *common carrier* or an *interactive computer service* to transport obscene matter in interstate or foreign commerce (1462)

♦ *Transport in interstate or foreign commerce* obscene matter for the purpose of sale or distribution (1465)

♦ Use a *facility or means of interstate or foreign commerce* (or an *interactive computer service* in or affecting such commerce) for the purpose of selling or distributing obscene matter (1465)

♦ *Distribute (wholesale or retail)* obscene matter that has already been shipped or transported in interstate or foreign commerce (18 USC 1466) [Person must also be "engaged in the business of" selling obscene matter.]

♦ Transmit obscene matter by means of *broadcast, cable, or satellite TV* (18 USC 1464, 1468)

♦ Transmit obscene *telephone* communications for commercial purposes (47 USC 223)

I wish to report a possible violation of Federal obscenity laws. I ask that you investigate and, if you find probable cause, that you take steps to initiate criminal obscenity or other appropriate legal proceedings against the individuals or businesses responsible.

In my opinion, the sexually oriented material described below may be obscene under the U.S. Supreme Court's three part obscenity test and in violation of Federal obscenity laws, in that a judge and jury may find that the material:

    1. When taken as a whole, appeals to the prurient interest in sex; and
    2. Depicts or describes hardcore sexual conduct in a patently offensive manner; and
    3. When taken as a whole, lacks serious literary, artistic, political, and scientific value.

I Am Reporting About:

☐ Mail porn (includes ads)   ☐ Retail establishment porn ("adult" or mainstream outlet)
☐ Dial-a-porn   ☐ Cable/satellite TV porn   ☐ Computer porn (including Web sites)

Name/address of company (e.g., store, cable TV operator, etc.) providing the material, and date observed:

_____

_____

(*If web site, give Web address [URL]; if telephone, the number; if TV, also provide channel name and number*)

Description of matter (video, DVD, pay-per-view film, magazine, audio message, paperback book, etc.) and title:

_____

_____

Which Depicts or Describes Sexual Conduct:

☐ Sexual Intercourse   ☐ Sadomasochism   ☐ Excretory Functions
☐ Masturbation   ☐ Sexual Bestiality   ☐ Lewd Exhibition of the Genitals
☐ Oral Sex   ☐ Anal Sex   ☐ Other _____

Please acknowledge receipt of this complaint.

CC: Morality in Media, 475 Riverside Drive, New York, NY 10115

APPENDIX 8:
USPS APPLICATION FOR LISTING AND/OR PROHIBITORY ORDER

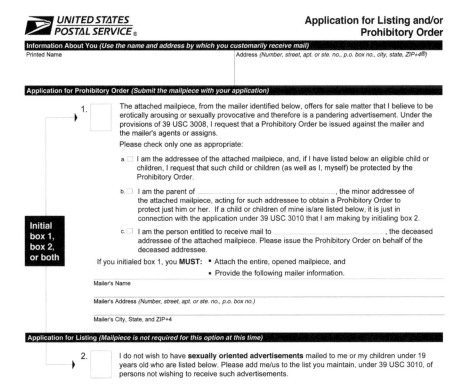

UNITED STATES POSTAL SERVICE®

Application for Listing and/or Prohibitory Order

Information About You *(Use the name and address by which you customarily receive mail)*

Printed Name

Address *(Number, street, apt. or ste. no., p.o. box no., city, state, ZIP+4®)*

Application for Prohibitory Order *(Submit the mailpiece with your application)*

1. ☐ The attached mailpiece, from the mailer identified below, offers for sale matter that I believe to be erotically arousing or sexually provocative and therefore is a pandering advertisement. Under the provisions of 39 USC 3008, I request that a Prohibitory Order be issued against the mailer and the mailer's agents or assigns.

Please check only one as appropriate:

a. ☐ I am the addressee of the attached mailpiece, and, if I have listed below an eligible child or children, I request that such child or children (as well as I, myself) be protected by the Prohibitory Order.

b. ☐ I am the parent of _____, the minor addressee of the attached mailpiece, acting for such addressee to obtain a Prohibitory Order to protect just him or her. If a child or children of mine is/are listed below, it is just in connection with the application under 39 USC 3010 that I am making by initialing box 2.

c. ☐ I am the person entitled to receive mail to _____, the deceased addressee of the attached mailpiece. Please issue the Prohibitory Order on behalf of the deceased addressee.

If you initialed box 1, you **MUST:** ▪ Attach the entire, opened mailpiece, and
▪ Provide the following mailer information.

Mailer's Name

Mailer's Address *(Number, street, apt. or ste. no., p.o. box no.)*

Mailer's City, State, and ZIP+4

Initial box 1, box 2, or both

Application for Listing *(Mailpiece is not required for this option at this time)*

2. ☐ I do not wish to have **sexually oriented advertisements** mailed to me or my children under 19 years old who are listed below. Please add me/us to the list you maintain, under 39 USC 3010, of persons not wishing to receive such advertisements.

Information About Your Children *(Age 18 and Under)*					
Children's Names			Date of Birth		
Last	First	Middle Initial	Month	Day	Year

Authorization

Signature of Adult Completing Form	Date

PS Form **1500**, July 2005 *(Page 2 of 5)* PSN 7530-03-000-7374   Processing Center

UNITED STATES
POSTAL SERVICE ®

Application for Listing and/or Prohibitory Order

Information About You *(Use the name and address by which you customarily receive mail)*

Printed Name

Address *(Number, street, apt. or ste. no., p.o. box no., city, state, ZIP+4®)*

Application for Prohibitory Order *(Submit the mailpiece with your application)*

1. The attached mailpiece, from the mailer identified below, offers for sale matter that I believe to be erotically arousing or sexually provocative and therefore is a pandering advertisement. Under the provisions of 39 USC 3008, I request that a Prohibitory Order be issued against the mailer and the mailer's agents or assigns.

Please check only one as appropriate:

a. ☐ I am the addressee of the attached mailpiece, and, if I have listed below an eligible child or children, I request that such child or children (as well as I, myself) be protected by the Prohibitory Order.

b. ☐ I am the parent of _____, the minor addressee of the attached mailpiece, acting for such addressee to obtain a Prohibitory Order to protect just him or her. If a child or children of mine is/are listed below, it is just in connection with the application under 39 USC 3010 that I am making by initialing box 2.

c. ☐ I am the person entitled to receive mail to _____, the deceased addressee of the attached mailpiece. Please issue the Prohibitory Order on behalf of the deceased addressee.

Initial box 1, box 2, or both

If you initialed box 1, you **MUST:** ▪ Attach the entire, opened mailpiece, and
▪ Provide the following mailer information.

Mailer's Name

Mailer's Address *(Number, street, apt. or ste. no., p.o. box no.)*

Mailer's City, State, and ZIP+4

Application for Listing *(Mailpiece is not required for this option at this time)*

2. I do not wish to have **sexually oriented advertisements** mailed to me or my children under 19 years old who are listed below. Please add me/us to the list you maintain, under 39 USC 3010, of persons not wishing to receive such advertisements.

Information About Your Children *(Age 18 and Under)*

Children's Names			Date of Birth		
Last	First	Middle Initial	Month	Day	Year

Authorization

Signature of Adult Completing Form

Important:
Keep this copy for your records.

Date

PS Form **1500,** July 2005, *(Page 3 of 5)* PSN 7530-03-000-7374

Applicant

Accepting Postal Service™ Employee:

Please review this form when it is turned in.

1. Is the form signed and dated?	☐ Yes	☐ No
2. Is the form legible?	☐ Yes	☐ No
3. Did the customer initial box 1 and/or 2?	☐ Yes	☐ No
4. If children are listed in the *Information About Your Children* section, are their birth dates included?	☐ Yes	☐ No
5. Are all children listed there age 18 or under?	☐ Yes	☐ No
6. Is the signature the same as the printed name on the application?	☐ Yes	☐ No

If the customer initialed box 1, answer the following questions:

1. Are the name and address of the mailer listed?	☐ Yes	☐ No
2. Did the customer give you the entire mailpiece (original, **NOT** a photocopy)?	☐ Yes	☐ No
3. Is the mailpiece opened?	☐ Yes	☐ No
4. Is one of box 1a, 1b, or 1c checked?	☐ Yes	☐ No

If you answered *NO* to any of these questions, do not forward!
(Refer to DMM® 508.8 or 508.9 as appropriate.)

Questions? For additional help, contact your district office or the Prohibitory Order Processing Center.

Accepting Office Name

Name of Accepting Employee

Signature of Accepting Employee

Send all completed forms NO LESS THAN weekly to:

PRICING AND CLASSIFICATION SERVICE CENTER
PO BOX 1500
NEW YORK NY 10008-1500

PS Form **1500,** July 2005 *(Page 4 of 5)* PSN 7530-03-000-7374

APPENDIX 9:
STATE CHILD PORNOGRAPHY STATUTES

STATE	STATUTE
Alabama	Ala. Code §§ 13A-12-191 et seq.; 13A-12-197
Alaska	Alaska Stat. §§ 11.61.125; 11.61.127
Arizona	Ariz. Rev. Stat. §§ 13-3552 et seq.
Arkansas	Ark. Code Ann. §§ 5-27-303(a); 5-27-304; 603
California	Cal. Penal Code §§ 311.3; 311.10; 311.11
Colorado	Colo. Rev. Stat. § 18-6-403
Connecticut	Conn. Gen. Stat. Ann. §§ 53a-196c; 53a-196d
Delaware	Del. Code Ann. tit. 11, §§ 1109; 1111
District of Columbia	D.C. Code §§ 22-3101 et seq.
Florida	Fla. Stat. Ann. ch. §§ 827.071; 847.0135; 847.0137
Georgia	Ga. Code Ann. §§ 16-12-100; 16-12-100.2
Hawaii	Haw. Rev. Stat. Ann. §§ 707-750 et seq.
Idaho	Idaho Code §§ 18-1507; 18-1507A(2)
Illinois	720 ILCS 5/11-20.1
Indiana	Ind. Code § 35-42-4-4
Iowa	Iowa Code § 728.12

STATE	STATUTE
Kansas	Kan. Stat. Ann. § 21-3516
Kentucky	Kentucky Rev. Stat. §§ 531.310 et seq.; 531.335; 531.340
Louisiana	La. Rev. Stat. § 14:81.1
Maine	Me. Rev. Stat., Title 17-A, §§ 282 et seq.
Maryland	Md. Code Ann. § 11-207
Massachusetts	Mass. Gen. Laws ch. 272, §§ 29A et seq.
Michigan	Mich. Stat. Ann. § 750.145c
Minnesota	Minn. Stat. Ann. § 617.246 et seq.
Mississippi	Miss. Code Ann. § 97-5-33
Missouri	Mo. Rev. Stat. §§ 573.010 et seq.
Montana	Mont. Code Ann. § 45-5-625
Nebraska	Neb. Rev. Stat. §§ 28-1463.03 et seq.
Nevada	Nev. Rev. Stat. §§ 200.710 et seq.
New Hampshire	N.H. Rev. Stat. Ann. § 649-A:3
New Jersey	N.J. Stat. § 2C:24-4
New Mexico	N.M. Stat. Ann. § 30-6A-3
New York	N.Y. Penal Law §§ 263.05 et seq.
North Carolina	N.C. Gen. Stat. §§ 14-190.16 et seq.
North Dakota	N.D. Cent. Code §§ 12.1-27.2-04.1 et seq.
Ohio	Ohio Rev. Code Ann. §§ 2907.321 et seq.
Oklahoma	21 Okla. Stat. §§ 1021 et seq.
Oregon	Ore. Rev. Stat. §§ 163.670 et seq.
Pennsylvania	18 Pa.C.S. § 6312
Rhode Island	R.I. Gen. Laws §§ 11-9-1.2 et seq.
South Carolina	S.C. Code Ann. §§ 16-15-395 et seq.

STATE	STATUTE
South Dakota	S.D. Codified Laws § 22-22-24.2
Tennessee	Tenn. Code Ann. §§ 39-17-1003 et seq.
Texas	Tex. Penal Code §§ 43.25 et seq.
Utah	Utah Code Ann. §§ 76-5a-2 et seq.
Vermont	Vt. Stat. Ann. tit, 13 §§ 2825 et seq.
Virginia	Va. Code Ann. §§ 18.2-374.1 et seq.
Washington	Wash. Rev. Code Ann. §§ 9.68A.040 et seq.
West Virginia	W. Va. Code §§ 61-8C-2 et seq.
Wisconsin	Wis. Stat. Ann. §§ 948.05; 948.12
Wyoming	Wyo. Stat. Ann. § 6-4-303

APPENDIX 10:
CYBER-TIPLINE ANNUAL REPORT TOTALS
(1/1/06–12/31/06)

TYPE OF INCIDENT	TOTAL REPORTS
Child Pornography (possession, manufacture, and distribution)	62,480
Child Prostitution	1,098
Child Sex Tourism	566
Child Sexual Molestation (not by a family member)	2,156
Online Enticement of Children for Sexual Acts	6,384
Unsolicited Obscene Material Sent to a Child	1,799
Misleading Domain Names	2,101
Grand Total	**76,584**

Source: National Center for Missing & Exploited Children.

APPENDIX 11:
FCC COMPLAINT FORM (475B)

Approved by OMB
3060-0874
Estimated time per response: 15 minutes

Federal Communications Commission
Washington, DC 20554

FCC Form 475B
Obscene, Profane, and/or Indecent Material Complaint Form

In order to process your complaint, the Commission needs the information marked below with an asterisk (*). Information not marked with an asterisk (*), if available, is also helpful.

Consumer Information:

*First Name: _____

Middle Initial: _____

*Last Name: _____

*Post Office : _____
 Box Number

*Street Address: _____

_____

(Either Street Address OR Post Office Box is required)

*City: _____

*State: _____

*Zip Code _____

E-Mail Address: _____

Daytime Telephone Number: _____

Program Information:

*(1) Date of Program: _____

*(2) Time of Program: _____

 (3) Network: _____

*(4) Call Sign, Channel **OR** Frequency of the station on which you viewed/heard the material: _____

*(5) City and State where program was viewed or heard: _____

(6) Name of Program or DJ/Personality/Song/Film: _____

*Please include below as many details about the program as possible in order to help the FCC determine whether the material was obscene, profane, and/or indecent (such as specific words, language, images, etc.).:

_____
_____
_____
_____
_____

You are not required to submit a transcript or an audiotape, videotape, CD/DVD or other recording in support of your complaint. Doing so, however, may help expedite the processing of your complaint. If you choose to submit a transcript you should send both this complaint and the transcript to The Federal Communications Commission, Consumer & Governmental Affairs Bureau, Consumer Inquiries and Complaints Division, 445 12th Street, SW, Washington, DC 20554. If you choose to submit an audiotape, videotape, CD/DVD or other recording, you should send both this complaint form and the recording to Federal Communications Commission, Consumer & Governmental Affairs Bureau, Consumer Inquiries and Complaints Division, 9300 East Hampton Drive, Capitol Heights, MD 20743. Any documentation of the programming becomes part of the Commission's records and cannot be returned.

For additional information, please see our Obscene, Profane, and Indecent Broadcasts Fact Sheet at http://www.fcc.gov/cgb/consumerfacts/obscene.pdf.

FCC NOTICE REQUIRED BY THE PRIVACY ACT AND PAPERWORK REDUCTION ACT

The Federal Communications Commission is authorized under the Communications Act of 1934, as amended, to collect the personal information that we request in this form. This form is used for complaints about obscene, profane and indecent programming. The public reporting for this collection of information is estimated to average 15 minutes per response, including the time for reviewing instructions, searching existing data sources, gathering and maintaining the required data, and completing and reviewing the collection of information. If you have any comments on this burden estimate, or how we can improve the collection and reduce the burden it causes you, please write to the Federal Communications Commission, AMD-PERM, Paperwork Reduction Project (3060-0874), Washington, DC 20554. We will also accept your comments regarding the Paperwork Reduction Act aspects of this collection via the Internet if you send them to Leslie.Smith@fcc.gov. PLEASE DO NOT SEND YOUR COMPLETED FORMS TO THIS ADDRESS.

Remember - You are not required to respond to a collection of information sponsored by the Federal government, and the government may not conduct or sponsor this collection, unless it displays a currently valid OMB control number or if we fail to provide you with this notice. This collection has been assigned an OMB control number of 3060-0874.

In addition, the information that consumers provide when filling out FCC Form 475B is covered by the system of records notice, FCC/CGB-1, Informal Complaints and Inquiries File (Broadcast, Common Carrier, and Wireless

Revised January 2006

Telecommunications Bureau Radio Services). The Commission is authorized to request this information from consumers under 47 U.S.C. 206, 208, 301, 303, 309(e), 312, 362, 364, 386, 507, and 51; and 47 CFR 1.711 *et seq.*

Under this system of records notice, FCC/CGB-1, the FCC may disclose information that consumers provide as follows: when a record in this system involves a complaint against a common carrier, the complaint is forwarded to the defendant carrier who must, within a prescribed time frame, either satisfy the complaint or explain to the Commission and the complainant its failure to do so; where there is an indication of a violation or potential violation of a statute, regulation, rule, or order, records from this system may be referred to the appropriate Federal, state, or local agency responsible for investigating or prosecuting a violation or for enforcing or implementing the statute, rule, regulation, or order; a record from this system may be disclosed to a Federal agency, in response to its request, in connection with the hiring or retention of an employee, the issuance of a security clearance, the reporting of an investigation of an employee, the letting of a contract, or the issuance of a license, grant or other benefit; a record on an individual in this system of records may be disclosed, where pertinent, in any legal proceeding to which the Commission is a party before a court or administrative body; a record from this system of records may be disclosed to the Department of Justice or in a proceeding before a court or adjudicative body when: the United States, the Commission, a component of the Commission, or, when represented by the government, an employee of the Commission is a party to litigation or anticipated litigation or has an interest in such litigation, and the Commission determines that the disclosure is relevant or necessary to the litigation; a record on an individual in this system of records may be disclosed to a Congressional office in response to an inquiry the individual has made to the Congressional office; and a record from this system of records may be disclosed to GSA and NARA for the purpose of records management inspections conducted under authority of 44 U.S.C. 2904 and 2906. Such disclosure shall not be used to make a determination about individuals.

In each of these cases, the FCC will determine whether disclosure of the information in this system of records notice is compatible with the purpose for which the records were collected. Furthermore, information in this system of records notice is available for public inspection after redaction of information that could identify the complainant or correspondent, *i.e.*, name, address and/or telephone number.

THE FOREGOING NOTICE IS REQUIRED BY THE PRIVACY ACT OF 1974, PUBLIC LAW 93-579, DECEMBER 31, 1974, 5 U.S.C. SECTION 552a(e)(3) AND THE PAPERWORK REDUCTION ACT OF 1995, PUBLIC LAW 104-13, OCTOBER 1, 1995, 44 U.S.C. SECTION 3507.

GLOSSARY

Ad Blocker—Software placed on a user's personal computer that prevents advertisements from being displayed on the Web.

Ad Network—Companies that purchase and place banner advertisements on behalf of their clients.

Affirmative Customization—Refers to a site's or an Internet Service Provider's use of personal data to tailor or modify the content or design of the site to specifications affirmatively selected by a particular individual.

Aggregate Information—Information that is related to a Web site visitor but is not about that individual personally, e.g., information kept about which pages on a Web site are most popular to a visitor but which cannot be traced to the individual personally.

American Civil Liberties Union (ACLU)—A nationwide organization dedicated to the enforcement and preservation of rights and civil liberties guaranteed by the federal and state constitutions.

Anonymity—A situation in which the user's true identity is not known.

Anonymizer—A service that prevents Web sites from seeing a user's Internet Protocol (IP) address. The service operates as an intermediary to protect the user's identity.

Anonymous Remailer—A special e-mail server that acts as a middleman and strips outgoing e-mail of all personally identifying information, then forwards it to its destination, usually with the IP address of the remailer attached.

Arrest—To deprive a person of his liberty by legal authority.

Authenticate—Process of verifying that the person attempting to send a message or access data is who he or she claims to be.

Authorize—To grant or deny a person access to data or systems.

Banner Ad—Advertisement for a product or company that is placed on a Web page in order to sell site visitors a good or service. Clicking on a banner will take the visitor to a site to learn more about that product or service.

Bestiality—The illegal act of sexual intercourse with an animal.

Bill of Rights—The first eight amendments to the United States Constitution.

Blocking Software—A computer program that allows parents, teachers, or guardians to "block" access to certain Web sites and other information available over the Internet.

Bookmark—A bookmark is an online function that lets the user access their favorite Web sites quickly.

Bowdlerize—The process of expurgating and revising literary works in order to remove objectionable language or ideas.

Browser—A browser is special software that allows the user to navigate several areas of the Internet and view a Web site.

Bulletin Board Systems—Electronic networks of computers that are connected by a central computer setup and operated by a system administrator or operator and are distinguishable from the Internet by their "dial-up" accessibility. BBS users link their individual computers to the central BBS computer by a modem that allows them to post messages, read messages left by others, trade information, or hold direct conversations. Access to a BBS can, and often is, privileged and limited to those users who have access privileges granted by the systems operator.

Burden of Proof—The duty of a party to substantiate an allegation or issue to convince the trier of fact as to the truth of their claim.

Cache—A place on the computer's hard drive where the browser stores information from pages or sites that the user has visited so that returning to those pages or sites is faster and easier.

Capacity—Capacity is the legal qualification concerning the ability of one to understand the nature and effects of one's acts.

CDA—Communications Decency Act of 1996.

Censorship—Review of publications, movies, plays and the like for the purpose of prohibiting the publication, distribution or production of material deemed objectionable as obscene, indecent or immoral.

Certiorari—A common law writ whereby a higher court requests a review of a lower court's records to determine whether any irregularities occurred in a particular proceeding.

Chat Room—A chat room is a place for people to converse online by typing messages to each other. A number of customers can be in the public chat rooms at any given time, which are monitored for illegal activity and even appropriate language by systems operators (SYSOP). The public chat rooms usually cover a broad range of topics such as entertainment, sports, game rooms, children only, etc.

Chat—Real-time text conversation between users in a chat room with no expectation of privacy. All chat conversation is accessible by all individuals in the chat room while the conversation is taking place.

Chief Justice—The presiding member of certain courts, which have more than one judge, e.g., the United States Supreme Court.

Child Abuse—Any form of cruelty to a child's physical, moral, or mental well-being.

Children's Online Privacy Protection Act (COPPA)—Law that prescribes a set of rules meant to protect children's privacy online.

Child Welfare—A generic term that embraces the totality of measures necessary for a child's well being; physical, moral, and mental.

CIPA—Children's Internet Protection Act of 2000.

Ciphertext—Scrambled, unreadable contents of an encrypted message or file.

Circuit—A judicial division of a state or the United States.

Circuit Court—One of several courts in a given jurisdiction.

Citation—A reference to a source of legal authority, such as a case or statute.

Civil Disobedience—The refusal to obey a law for the purpose of demonstrating its unfairness.

Common Law—Common law is the system of jurisprudence that originated in England and was later applied in the United States. The common law is based on judicial precedent rather than statutory law.

Conclusion of Fact—A conclusion reached by natural inference and based solely on the facts presented.

Conclusion of Law—A conclusion reached through the application of rules of law.

Conclusive Evidence—Evidence that is incontrovertible.

Consent—Explicit permission, given to a Web site by a visitor, to handle personal information in specified ways. "Informed consent" implies that the company fully discloses its information practices prior to obtaining personal data or permission to use it.

Conspiracy—A scheme by two or more persons to commit a criminal or unlawful act.

Conspirator—One of the parties involved in a conspiracy.

Constitution—The fundamental principles of law that frame a governmental system.

Constitutional Right—Refers to the individual liberties granted by the constitution of a state or the federal government.

Cookie—When the user visits a site, a notation may be fed to a file known as a "cookie" in their computer for future reference. If the user revisits the site, the "cookie" file allows the Web site to identify the user as a "return" guest and offers the user products tailored to their interests or tastes.

Cookie Buster—Software that is designed to block the placement of cookies by ad networks and Web sites thus preventing companies from tracking a user's activity.

COPA—Child Online Protection Act of 1998.

Court—The branch of government responsible for the resolution of disputes arising under the laws of the government.

Criminal Impersonation—As it pertains to identity theft, means to knowingly assume a false or fictitious identity or capacity, and in that identity or capacity, doing any act with intent to unlawfully gain a benefit or injure, or defraud another.

Culpable—Referring to conduct, it is that which is deserving of moral blame.

Cyberspace—Cyberspace is another name for the Internet.

Data Spill—The result of a poorly designed form on a Web site which may cause an information leak to web servers of other companies, such as an ad network or advertising agency.

Decrypt—To decode data from its protected, scrambled form so it can be read.

Defamation—The publication of an injurious statement about the reputation of another.

Defendant—In a civil proceeding, the party responding to the complaint.

Defense—Opposition to the truth or validity of the plaintiff's claims.

Delinquent—A juvenile of not more than a specified age who has violated criminal laws or has engaged in disobedient, indecent or immoral conduct, and is in need of treatment, rehabilitation, or supervision.

Digital Certificate—Process using encryption technology whereby a document can be digitally stamped or certified as to its place of origin, and a certification authority supports and legitimizes the certificates.

Digital Signature—A digital certification or stamp that uses encryption technology to authenticate that an individual's signature is legitimate.

Digital storm—Analytic tools currently being developed by the FBI to sift and link data from disparate sources.

Directories—Indexes of Web pages organized by subject.

District Attorney—An officer of a governmental body with the duty to prosecute those accused of crimes.

Download—A download is the transfer of files or software from a remote computer to the user's computer.

Downstream Data Use—Refers to companies' practice of disclosing personal information collected from users to other parties downstream to facilitate a transaction.

Due Process Rights—All rights that are of such fundamental importance as to require compliance with due process standards of fairness and justice.

Dynamic IP Address—An IP address that changes every time a user logs on, or dials-up, to a computer.

Encryption—The scrambling of digital information so that it is unreadable to the average user. A computer must have "digital keys" to unscramble and read the information.

Encryption Software—Often used as a security measure, encryption software scrambles data so that it is unreadable to interceptors without the appropriate information to read the data.

Entrapment—In criminal law, refers to the use of trickery by the police to induce the defendant to commit a crime for which he or she has a predisposition to commit.

E-mail—E-mail is computer-to-computer messages between one or more individuals via the Internet.

Ethernet—A commonly used networking technology that links computers together.

Ethernet Adapter Address—The personal name of the Ethernet card in a user's computer.

Fairness Doctrine—An FCC regulation requiring radio and television broadcasters to provide coverage of issues of public importance and to present contrasting views.

Felony—A crime of a graver or more serious nature than those designated as misdemeanors.

File Transfer Protocol (FTP)—A way to transfer files from one computer to another.

Filter—Filter is software the user can buy that lets the user block access to Web sites and content that they may find unsuitable.

Fine—A financial penalty imposed upon a defendant.

Firewall—A hardware or software device that controls access to computers on a Local Area Network (LAN). It examines all traffic routed between the two networks—inbound and outbound—to see if it meets certain criteria. If it does, it is routed between the networks, otherwise it is stopped. It can also manage public access to private networked resources such as host applications.

First Amendment—The First Amendment of the United States Constitution protects the right to freedom of religion and freedom of expression from government interference.

Fornication—Unlawful sexual intercourse between two unmarried persons.

Fraud—Fraud is a false representation of a matter of fact, whether by words or by conduct, by false or misleading allegations, or by concealment of that which should have been disclosed, which deceives and is intended to deceive another so that he shall act upon it to his legal injury.

Globally Unique Identifier (GUID)—A unique code used to identify a computer, user, file, etc., for tracking purposes.

Hardware—The computer and related machines such as scanners and printers.

Harmful to Minors—A term used to describe any picture, image, graphic image file, or other visual depiction that: (a) taken as a whole and with respect to minors, appeals to a prurient interest in nudity, sex, or excretion; (b) depicts, describes, or represents, in a patently offensive way with respect to what is suitable for minors, an actual or simulated sexual act or sexual contact, actual or simulated normal or perverted sexual acts, or a lewd exhibition of the genitals; and (c) taken as a whole, lacks serious literary, artistic, political, or scientific value as to minors.

Host Name—Each computer is given a name, which typically includes the user name and the organizational owner of the computer.

Home Page—The first page or document web users see when connecting to a web server or when visiting a Web site.

Hyperlink—An image or portion of text on a Web page that is linked to another Web page. The user clicks on the link to go to another Web page or another place on the same page.

Hypertext Markup Language (HTML)—The standard language used for creating documents on the Internet.

Hypertext Transfer Protocol (HTTP)—The standard language that computers connected to the Internet use to communicate with each other.

Ignorance—Lack of knowledge.

Ignorantia Legis Non Excusat—Latin for "Ignorance of the law is no excuse." Although an individual may not think an act is illegal, the act is still punishable.

Illegal—Against the law.

Indecency—Expression that is morally indelicate, improper, offensive or tending to be obscene.

Injunction—A judicial remedy either requiring a party to perform an act, or restricting a party from continuing a particular act.

Instant messa ge (IP)—A chat-like technology on an online service that notifies a user when another person is online, allowing for simultaneous communication.

Internet—The Internet is the universal network that allows computers to talk to other computers in words, text, graphics, and sound, anywhere in the world.

Internet Access Service—A service that enables users to access content, information, electronic mail, or other services offered over the Internet, and may also include access to proprietary content, information, and other services as part of a package of services offered to consumers.

Internet Information Location tool—A service that refers or links users to an online location on the World Wide Web. Such term includes directories, indices, references, pointers, and hypertext links.

Internal Protocol (IP)—The standards by which computers talk to each other over the Internet.

Internet Service Provider (ISP)—A service that allows the user to connect to the Internet.

IP Address—A number or series of numbers that identify a computer linked to the Internet and which is generally written as four numbers separated by periods, e.g., 12.24.36.48.

JavaScript—A programming language used to add features to Web pages in order to make the Web site more interactive.

Junk E-mail—Junk e-mail is unsolicited commercial e-mail also known as "spam."

Keyword—A word the user enters into a search engine to begin the search for specific information or Web sites.

Kidnapping—The illegal taking of a person against his or her will.

Lewd—Obscene, lustful, indecent, or lascivious.

Lewdness—Gross indecency so notorious as to tend to corrupt community's morals.

Liability—Liability refers to one's obligation to do or refrain from doing something, such as the payment of a debt.

Libel—A form of unprotected speech involving the false and malicious publication of defamatory words that are written or broadcast.

Links—Links are highlighted words on a Web site that allow the user to connect to other parts of the same Web site or to other Web sites.

Listserve—An online mailing list that allows individuals or organizations to send e-mail to groups of people at one time.

Local Area Network (LAN)—A computer network limited to the immediate area, usually the same building or floor of a building.

Mann Act—A federal statute prohibiting the transportation of a female across state lines for the purpose of prostitution.

Media Access Control—The unique Ethernet card ID number found in network computers.

Minor—A person who has not yet reached the age of legal competence, which is designated as 18 in most states.

Misdemeanor—Criminal offenses that are less serious than felonies and carry lesser penalties.

Modem—A modem is an internal or external device that connects the computer to a phone line and, if the user wishes, to a company that can link the user to the Internet.

Mouse—A small device attached to the computer by a cord, which lets the user give commands to the computer by clicking.

Obscene—Objectionable or offensive to accepted standards of decency.

Obscene Material—Material which lacks serious literary, artistic, political or scientific value and, taken as a whole, appeals to the prurient interest and, as such, is not protected by the free speech guarantee of the First Amendment.

Obscenity—The character or quality of being obscene; conduct tending to corrupt the public morals by its indecency or lewdness.

Offense—Any misdemeanor or felony violation of the law for which a penalty is prescribed.

Online profiling—The practice of aggregating information about consumers' preferences and interests, gathered primarily by tracking their online movements and actions, with the purpose of creating targeted advertisement using the resulting profiles.

Online Service—An online service is an ISP with added information, entertainment, and shopping features.

Operating system—The main program that runs on a computer.

Operator—The person who is responsible for maintaining and running a Web site.

Opinion—The reasoning behind a court's decision.

Opt-In—Refers to when a user gives explicit permission for a company to use personal information for marketing purposes.

Opt-Out—Refers to when a user prohibits a company from using personal information for marketing purposes.

Original Jurisdiction—The jurisdiction of a court to hear a matter in the first instance.

Overrule—A holding in a particular case is overruled when the same court, or a higher court, in that jurisdiction, makes an opposite ruling in a subsequent case on the identical point of law ruled upon in the prior case.

Packet—Term for the small bundles of digital information passed between users and sites.

Packet Sniffer—A software tool used to track the packets of information sent to and from a computer.

Parens Patriae—Latin for "parent of his country." Refers to the role of the state as guardian of legally disabled individuals.

Password—A personal code that the user selects to access their account with their ISP.

Personally Identifiable Information (PII)—Refers to information such as name, mailing address, phone number, or e-mail address.

Ping—A short message sent by a computer across a network to another computer confirming that the target computer is up and running.

Platform for Privacy Preferences Project (P3P)—A proposed browser feature that would analyze privacy policies and allow a user to control what personal information is revealed to a particular site.

Police Power—The power of the state to restrict private individuals in matters relating to public health, safety, and morality, and to impose such other restrictions as may be necessary to promote the welfare of the general public.

Pornographic—That which is of or pertaining to obscene literature; obscene; licentious.

Precedent—A previously decided case that is recognized as authority for the disposition of future cases.

Preference Data—Data, which may be collected by a site or a service provider about an individual's likes and dislikes.

Pretexting—The practice of fraudulently obtaining personal financial information, such as account numbers and balances, by calling financial institutions under the pretext of being a customer.

Pretty Good Privacy (PGP)—A widely used encryption software.

Prior Restraint—Legal action taken to suppress speech prior to its expression rather than punishing it on the basis of what was said.

Private Key—A data file assigned to a single individual to use in decrypting messages previously encrypted through use of that person's key.

Privacy Policy—A privacy policy is a statement on a Web site describing what information about the user is collected by the site and how it is used; also known as a privacy statement or privacy notice.

Privacy Seal Program—A program that certifies a site's compliance with the standards of privacy protection. Only those sites that comply with the standards are able to note certification.

Proxy Server—A system that caches items from other servers to speed up access.

Prurient Interest—The shameful and morbid interest in nudity and sex.

Pseudonymity—A situation in which the user has taken on an assumed identity.

Public Defender—A lawyer hired by the government to represent an indigent person accused of a crime.

Public Forum—Refers to a digital entity such as a bulletin board, public directory, or commercial CD-ROM directory, where personal user data may be distributed by a site or a service provider.

Public Key—A data file assigned to a specific person but which others can use to send the person encrypted messages. Because public keys don't contain the components necessary to decrypt messages, they are safe to distribute to others.

Query String—The extended string of a URL after the standard Web site address.

Rape—The unlawful sexual intercourse with a female person without her consent.

Rational Basis Test—The constitutional analysis of a law to determine whether it has a reasonable relationship to some legitimate government objective so as to uphold the law.

Sanction—A form of punishment.

Screen Name—A screen name is the name the user selects to be known by when the user communicates online.

Search and Seizure—The search by law enforcement officials of a person or place in order to seize evidence to be used in the investigation and prosecution of a crime.

Search Engine—A function that lets the user search for information and Web sites. Search engines or search functions may be found on many Web sites.

Search Warrant—A judicial order authorizing and directing law enforcement officials to search a specified location for specific items or individuals.

Secondary Use—Refers to using personal information collected for one purpose for a second, unrelated purpose.

Secure Anonymous Remailer—Web sites that will strip a consumer's identifying information so they can surf other Web sites and send e-mail anonymously.

Server—A host computer that stores information and/or software programs and makes them available to users of other computers.

Slander—Spoken words that are damaging to the reputation of another.

Spam—E-mail from a company or charity that is unsolicited and sent to many people at one time, usually for advertising purposes; also known as junk e-mail.

Static IP Address—An IP address that remains the same each time a user logs on or dials up a server.

Supreme Court—In most jurisdictions, the Supreme Court is the highest appellate court, including the federal court system.

Testify—The offering of a statement in a judicial proceeding, under oath and subject to the penalty of perjury.

Testimony—The sworn statement make by a witness in a judicial proceeding.

Third Party Ad Server—Companies that put banner advertising on Web sites that are generally not owned by that advertiser.

Third Party Cookie—A cookie that is placed by a party other than the user or the Web site being viewed, such as advertising or marketing groups who are trying to gather data on general consumer use third party cookies.

Trace Route—The course that a packet travels across the Internet from one computer to another.

Tracker GIF—Electronic images, usually not visible to site visitors, that allow a Web site to count those who have visited that page or to access certain cookies; also known as a "Clear GIF."

Trial—The judicial procedure whereby disputes are determined based on the presentation of issues of law and fact. Issues of fact are decided by the trier of fact, either the judge or jury, and issues of law are decided by the judge.

Trial Court—The court of original jurisdiction over a particular matter.

TRUSTe—An online privacy seal program that certifies eligible Web sites, holding sites to baseline privacy standards. TRUSTe requires its licensees to implement certain fair information practices and to submit to various types of compliance monitoring in order to display a privacy seal on their Web sites.

Trustmark—An online seal awarded by TRUSTe to Web sites that agree to post their privacy practices openly via privacy statements, as well as adhere to enforcement procedures that ensure that those privacy promises are met.

Unconstitutional—Refers to a statute which conflicts with the United States Constitution rendering it void.

Undue Influence—The exertion of improper influence upon another for the purpose of destroying that person's free will in carrying out a particular act.

Uniform Resource Locator (URL)—The address that lets the user locate a particular site. For example, http://www.ftc.gov is the URL for the Federal Trade Commission. Government URLs end in ".gov" and non-profit organizations and trade associations end in ".org." Commercial companies generally end in ".com," although additional suffixes or domains may be used as the number of Internet businesses grows.

Unique Identifiers—Non-financial identifiers issued for purposes of consistently identifying the individual.

Unreasonable Search and Seizure—A search and seizure that has not met the constitutional requirements under the Fourth and Fourteenth Amendment.

Upload—Copying or sending data or documents from one computer to another computer.

Use—Refers to the practice of collecting and using personal data internally, within the company or organization, for both administrative and marketing purposes.

User—An individual on whose behalf a service is accessed and for which personal data exists.

V-Chip—A microchip installed in television sets for the specific purpose of allowing parents to screen out undesirable programming.

Verdict—The definitive answer given by the jury to the court concerning the matters of fact committed to the jury for their deliberation and determination.

Verifiable Parental Consent—A type of parental consent obtained by a Web site to collect information from children under age 13 which must be verifiable, e.g., by written permission or a credit card number.

Vice Crimes—Illegal activities that offend the moral standards of the community, such as gambling and prostitution.

Virus—A file maliciously planted in the user's computer that can damage files and disrupt their system.

Void—Having no legal force or binding effect.

Void for Vagueness—The term given a criminal statute which is so vague that persons of normal intelligence do not comprehend its application, thus rendering it void.

Waiver—Waiver refers to an intentional and voluntary surrender of a known right.

Warrant—An official order directing that a certain act be undertaken, such as an arrest.

Warrantless Arrest—An arrest carried out without a warrant.

Web Bug—A graphic in a Web site or enhanced e-mail message that enables a third party to monitor who is reading the page or message.

Web Site—A Web site is an Internet destination where the user can look at and retrieve data. All the Web sites in the world, linked together, make up the World Wide Web or the "Web."

BIBLIOGRAPHY AND ADDITIONAL RESOURCES

American Civil Liberties Union (Date Visited: October 2008) http://www.aclu.org/

Attorney General's Commission on Pornography Final Report. Attorney General's Commission on Pornography. Washington, DC: GPO, 1988.

Black's Law Dictionary, Fifth Edition. St. Paul, MN: West Publishing Company, 1979.

Entertainment Software Rating Board (Date Visited: October 2008) http://www.esrb.org/

EPCAT International (Date Visited: October 2008) http://www.ecpat.net/

Federal Bureau of Investigation (Date Visited: October 2008) http://www.fbi.gov/

Federal Communications Com mission (Date Visited: October 2008) http://www.fcc.gov/

The Henry J. Kaiser Family Foundation (Date Visited: October 2008) http://www.kff.org/

Morality In Media, Inc. (Date Visited: October 2008) http://www.obscenitycrimes.org/

Motion Picture Association of America (Date Visited: October 2008) http://www.mpaa.org/

National Center for Missing and Exploited Children (Date Visited: October 2008) http://www.missingkids.com/

The National Obscenity Law Center (Date Visited: October 2008) http://www.moralityinmedia.org/nolc/index.htm/

Pause Parent Play (Date Visited: October 2008) http://www.pauseparentplay.org/

TV Parental Guidelines (Date Visited: October 2008) http://www.tvguidelines.org/

United States Department of Justice (Date Visited: October 2008) http://www.usdoj.gov/

United States Office of the Attorney General (Date Visited: October 2008) http://www.usdoj.gov/ag/

United States Postal Service (Date Visited: October 2008) http://www.usps.com/